G.P.S. Guide
For Athletes and Those Who Surround Them

How to Empower Your Sports **G**oals, Navigate the **P**rocess, and **S**teer toward Success

G.P.S. Guide
For Athletes and Those Who Surround Them

How to Empower Your Sports **G**oals, Navigate the **P**rocess, and **S**teer toward Success

Michael McGinnis, J.D.

All rights reserved. No part of this book may be reproduced, stored, or transmitted by any means, whether auditory, graphic, mechanical, or electronic without written permission of both publisher and author, except in the case of brief excerpts used in critical articles and reviews. Unauthorized reproduction of any part of this work is illegal and is punishable by law.

ISBN 1-944662-34-9

Publishing date: March 2019

Cover Design by Michael Scott, MASgraphicarts.com

Dedication

To my sons, Isaac and Bodhi, the best men I know—the individuals who make me want to be the best man I can possibly be. I love my fiery, fun, and friendly future entrepreneurs. All I do, and all I am, is for you. Love your papa bear, papa Batman, papa dinosaur McGinnis. Be great… and it always starts with being grateful.

Of course this book is also dedicated to my wonderful wife who is the fuel to my flame and allows me to continue to press forward on this journey of life because she walks with me side by side, believing in me even when I may not believe in myself.

To my mother, grandmother (RIP), and brothers for helping mold and shape me into the man I am today. I am grateful for your guidance and support.

Table of Contents

Dedication v

Foreword vii

Preface xii

Introduction xxi

Part I GOALS

GOAL ONE Find Your Geolocation 1

GOAL TWO Learn the Waypoints on How to Navigate the Current Process 25

GOAL THREE How to Accelerate Toward Maximum Benefits 61

GOAL FOUR Learn Why the Current Process has Veered Off-Track 87

Part II PROCESS

GOAL FIVE Re-calculating the Process toward a Culture of Empowerment 111

GOAL SIX Implementing the New Process to Reach Your Destination! 135

Part III SUCCESS

GOAL SEVEN The Empowered Mindset Routes to Success 149

GOAL EIGHT Stay on Course toward Success with Mental Strength 169

Conclusion 183

About The Author 187

Acknowledgements 189

How To Order 191

Foreword

I met Michael several years ago. We were introduced by a mutual friend who had told me that Michael and I would work very well together because he was not only an athlete but also a law student working in sports law with the intention of becoming a sports agent. Michael and I talked on the phone several times, and that ultimately resulted in me flying to Phoenix which is where he was living at the time with his new spouse. We hit it off famously and I came away from our meeting thinking, *this guy is wonderful. Very genuine. Very thoughtful. Very compassionate.* I had never witnessed a sports professional so sincere in wanting to do the right thing. And not just for athletes, for humanity.

I observed Michael's strength of character most notably when a high school senior moved unexpectedly from Tennessee to California, and was languishing in the school's sports program. The senior was an extremely talented basketball player in his previous environment, and had been promised a great senior season in a particular high school in the L.A. area. I called Michael. "Hey, can you help me out with this young man?" He was quick to step to the plate and spent a couple of weeks helping this independent high school senior, along with his very determined parents, navigate their way around Los Angeles, finding him a place to stay, and advising him on his athletic path. Michael went above and beyond the status quo because of his passion for helping athletes.

Michael McGinnis J.D.

☙ ❧

Over the past several decades I've built nine businesses and throughout my business career I've always been very involved in athletics. As a participant, I was a pretty fair athlete, not world class, but very competitive. I played basketball and golf, up to the university level, and finally, and reluctantly, gave them up to be a better student. I recognized I would never make it on the "big" stage. As my children grew up, I was involved in both of their athletic activities. Both my children were involved in athletics at some level and in some sports. Over the past twenty-plus years, using the lessons and principles I've learned along the way being exposed to athletics at many levels, I've mentored many athletes, probably over two hundred, many of whom have done very well; in fact several of them play in the NBA and NFL. Whether as high school, D-1 college, or professional athletes, I talk to these guys regularly as an athlete and as an individual, in their relationships, their sports, or their post-sports plans, and I work with them on five key ingredients of being a leader.

I grew up in a typical Middle America small town middle school and high school, yet I've always had a real affinity for working with urban kids. I've sponsored urban basketball and have worked with inner city athletes. These kids are so conditioned to following the coach, that when the coach tells them something, they just do it blindly instead of thinking for themselves. This is honestly essential to success as a team. However, this is also why I believe Michael's book is so important. He emphasizes the need for not only the athlete but all the people who surround the athlete to empower themselves, to take ownership of themselves and their lives.

I also stress that same point to all athletes I mentor. I tell them, "You know, the team is hiring you for your talent but while you may play for one pro team, the second you aren't performing to their standard, they're going to put you back in the stable and go after the next young racehorse whose step is quicker and whose agility or skills may be higher.

In this book, Michael also helps athletes and those who surround them to better manage their mental game. Winning the mental game is not only about recovering after a defeat or injury, it's handling the public attention, personal relationships, monetary success, and media frenzy. This is what commonly happens when you're a high-profile athlete, no matter what level you're playing at: You go to dinner. Before, during, and after your dinner, people are coming up to you, wanting to say hello, wanting your autograph, or just to shake your hand. They might even be bold enough to sit down at your table and ask for a mini photo shoot, or blast you out on one of the live social media channels. You're thinking, *Really man? Can't you see I'm trying to enjoy dinner with my friends? Are you really that lame?* But you know that if you're even "perceived" to be rude, that person is going to tell all their friends, it could reach the media, and all of a sudden you have negative press. Yes, it happens that fast! By the time the story hits the media, the headline reads: Mr. Athlete attacks a fan while at dinner…blah…blah.

I tell athletes all the time, "You are a leader whether you want to be or not. You're in a glass bubble, and people are going to emulate your behavior, good or bad. If you're a high school star basketball player you're likely to get all the good-looking girls following you around. The younger guys see this "stardom" and are going to want to *be* you. If they see you treating others disrespectfully, they'll emulate you. If you act up and embarrass others and cause problems, those who follow you will emulate you. So I repeat, you're a leader whether you like it or not, so BE the kind of leader others will want to follow, BE a leader who will lead others to become better human beings.

ଓ ଞ

I use what I call the Four S's when I talk to athletes. The first S is Struggle. Every single one of us struggles in some point or in some way. The second S is Satisfaction. We're treading water, not making much progress, but we're not falling backwards either. The third S is Success. We're making forward progress, we're getting ahead in life, and the skies are a lot bluer and brighter. The first three S's are all about an individual. The fourth S is Significance which involves giving back to others, empowering them to become successful in their own right. Michael's GPS model blends beautifully with the four S's as he lays out a success map of how to navigate through the current process while sharing a new, empowered, better process going forward. Most athletes are more crisis management-oriented than proactive management-oriented, but if they get hold of this book, it could really have an impact on how they conduct themselves and the level of success they experience during and after their sports career.

As for those who surround the athlete—parents, coaches, friends, players, agents, and other sports professionals—you need to ensure your athlete is equipped with success and empowerment tools, physically, mentally, emotionally, and even spiritually. I liken it to wearing armor. Youth want a sexy, classy, fun message. Not the kind of message that requires them to take off their armor, be vulnerable and accept raw coaching, criticism, or suggestions for improvement, and really get serious. I say this because athletes, on the field and in general, wear armor. They spend a lot of time and effort polishing the exterior of that armor, yet there's so much pressure pressing and pushing from the outside that it's easy for the armor to get dented and dinged. And then there's the internal pressure that pushes on the armor from the inside out. If there's not an internal framework behind that armor, then any time a fracture occurs, the armor instantly flattens and the athlete falls apart. The core of Michael's message is equipping the athlete and those who surround him to strengthen the external *and* internal armor so it shines brightly and lights the way for a successful life.

Mark Allen
Serial Entrepreneur & Mentor to Professional Athletes

Michael McGinnis J.D.

Preface

Every book gives you a reason to either pick it up and read it, or put it back down and forget about it. You know those books that you can't wait to read? They are the ones that scream your name every time you walk by. They call out to you, almost audibly, *Pick me up and read me*! They grab your attention and keep it aflame through the last page. You also know those books that repel you to do anything else *but* read? Every time you pick up the "forget about it" book, you start thinking how you'd rather be dusting, or doing laundry, mowing the lawn, or maybe even getting your teeth cleaned. Those books are the ones that collect dust. They get shuffled from place to place, and finally get tossed in your donation bin, never to be seen again.

With that said, why should you read THIS book? Why is THIS book a *pick me up and read me* book? Here's why: You need to read this book if you're anywhere on the conveyor belt within the sports world. Whether you're a parent of a Pee Wee, Little League, AAU, or travel ball student-athlete, or a middle school or high school athlete with a goal to make it to the big leagues, or a coach coaching youth football, wondering how you can better guide your players through the sports process, or an agent or other type of sports professional seeking the best information to provide your clients, this book lays out the process for you and shows you new ways to think about how you navigate within that process. You'll want to keep this book as a handy reference guide so you can refer back to it time and again.

Let me ask my original question in a little different way. Why should you listen to me? After all, you probably don't know me. Perhaps you're wondering what qualifies me to write an authoritative book such as this. Besides being an industry insider and intimately knowing and understanding the process and how it works, I grew up witnessing first-hand the blue-collar world of working hard and not smart. I was born and raised in the Midwest town of Dayton, Ohio, and in my town it was all too common to succumb to that "work hard and collect a paycheck" lifestyle; allowing someone else to determine your wealth, telling you to go "earn" a piece of paper, and going into work for eight to nine hours a day. Please don't misunderstand me. I don't say that to make fun of where I'm from, and I don't make fun of individuals who live that life, but I learned and witnessed first-hand how difficult and unfulfilling that life was, and I always aspired for more.

The book you hold in your hands (or on your phone or tablet) was born not only from my education and experience, but from watching others live a life of status quo, thinking there was nothing better out there than the daily grind of playing by someone else's rules.

Don't get me wrong, I have an amazing mother, and she always provided for me and my two brothers—she was our backbone. She and my grandmother were both the backbones of my family, and they worked extremely hard for us. Although I understood the working life, I always wanted more because I knew I was capable of doing great things and I had within me an overwhelming desire to provide the world tremendous value. I stayed near home and went to the University of Dayton where I received my Sports

Management degree with a minor in Entrepreneurship and minor in Communications. It was an amazing experience and I loved my time there. I joined the Kappa Alpha Psi Fraternity Incorporated, and met some of my best friends; men that I will know, God willing, until the end of my days on this earth.

While at UD I also met my wonderful wife, Adriana, which made it even more of an amazing experience. After my time at UD I went to Arizona and headed into law school, because at the time I thought everyone wanted a 22-year-old sports agent, although I quickly learned that wasn't the case. So I hightailed it to the Southwest because it was the farthest from the Midwest—it was time to flap my wings and see the world and receive my Juris Doctorate.

But that's also where I went to fail.

I never loved school. I had no desire to pursue a Doctorate yet I knew I needed to do *something* in order to accomplish what I wanted to accomplish. During my time in Law School, my grandmother who was extremely instrumental in my life became very sick during my first year of law school, and to add to that, I was already struggling being away from home, being apart from my girlfriend (now wife), and being on my own for the first time in my life.

So I hit a lot of roadblocks. I struggled. It was tough. My grandmother's health took a very bad turn so I went back and saw her toward the spring of that first year, and she actually ended up passing away a couple weeks before I took my final exams. So it was a very, very tough time. But it's how I became the man I am today, because I was able to rise through all those tough times and chart a course for where I wanted to go even if the course required me to do things that maybe I wasn't comfortable with. I rose to the occasion, accepted the challenge and continued to navigate.

At the conclusion of my first year in law school I actually ended up proposing to my girlfriend, so I think the challenge of being away from home, and the struggle, the sacrifice, helped prepare me for the challenges and sacrifices I would soon be making as I prepared to receive a Doctorate degree and take on an exorbitant amount of debt to the tune of $280,000. However, looking back, I wouldn't change all that struggle for anything in the world.

After getting the degree, getting married and starting a family, I realized once again that no one really wanted a 25-year-old sports agent. Losing my grandmother was significant, but one of the most draining points in my life was when I was 25; I had just graduated law school at the pace any average human being could, because again, I'm no boy genius. I put in the work and I got the result. But that last month after I graduated law school, I sat and watched Netflix for a month. My fiancée would go to work; I was just there.

I knew I would be taking the Arizona Bar Exam but not until the following February, but in the meantime I thought the world was going to open up magically and I would instantly become a great success because I had two pieces of paper that said I was a college graduate and a law school graduate. And there I was, at home watching Netflix. My thinking reflected my belief that everything would magically work out because I did everything by the book. I worked hard. I followed the Midwest culture in which I was ingrained. It was at that point in time when I finally realized that hard work doesn't always lead to success, by my measure of success. I had to become active and engage.

I'd been getting some agency experience. I kind of glossed over that, but I previously had been working with two sports agencies. During my second year of law school, I finally was given an opportunity to be an intern for free at a sports agency down there in the Scottsdale, Arizona area. It took four and a half years just to get that year of free experience.

But through that success of that free year of experience, I was able to then prove my value to where I was given an opportunity to pretty much, hey, come on board and be a part of this. And in the process of that, I'd always aspired to work in basketball, because being an African-American male, I felt the calling and the need for someone who looked like me to be an advocate for those individuals that I felt were given some of what I like to say was misguided advice. These advisers let them think that the world was their oyster and that no matter what happened to them, if they kept throwing that ball through the hoop, the world would just miraculously come together for them.

I felt like I identified with that because, again, I was on my path to success, and I felt like you couldn't tell me anything. I was succeeding. I was going to make it happen no matter what. But that isn't the reality. Just because you do certain things, and people hold you up on a pedestal, that doesn't mean you automatically receive your definition of success. But still, in the process, I was getting closer and was able to also, during my second year of law school, work with a baseball agent and a basketball agency.

The first year of law school they scare you to death, the second they work you to death, and the third year they bore you to death. So I was going through a very tough time mentally, working extremely hard on the academic side, and then taking on two immense challenges in the industry I aspired to work in, but I survived it. I survived it and I made it through.

My fiancée (soon-to-be-wife) and I were expecting our first child at the time which was a very scary time for me because I didn't grow up with a father. I only knew how difficult it was for my mother; I knew full well that kids are a responsibility that require you to always put their needs and requirements first. They come first when you're tired, they come first when you're financially hurting, and they come first when you want to go do something else. As a man who grew up with the mentality of "pull yourself up by the bootstraps" I knew I was to be the provider for my wife and kids—I mean, that was ingrained in me within the Midwest culture. I was scared because here I was walking out of school with a piece of paper that elicited the feeling of *Hurray, I've arrived* yet I had a school bill that had to get paid and a fiancée who was expecting a baby.

I decided to take a job opportunity to work on behalf of the Department of Defense and work and support the Air Force out here in the Southern California area, and learn how to negotiate and write contracts, because that was the only piece of the agent puzzle that I had not directly worked on. I knew how to recruit, I knew how to scout, I knew how to build relationships, and I loved talking to people; the stuff you envision when you think of sports agents. I now had an undergraduate degree and a law degree but I needed the meat and potatoes experience of the industry. I got that quicker than I realized.

Through the years I've worked on contracts in the billions of dollars, larger than some of the most successful agents in the industry today. I was working on those types of contracts in my mid-20s and that experience empowered and equipped me to go out and properly serve and advocate and provide the guidance and support that I feel that athletes and their families needed. My career choice to enter the sports agent industry was fueled by the fact that there was a need I wanted to fulfill. I witnessed the necessity of education and genuine care in the lives of young athletes and I don't know if my desire stems from not having had a father in my life, but what I do know is how instrumental it is to have a strong male presence in your corner. I definitely had the presence of my mother, grandmother, and older brother, so I don't want to by any means say that I was a lone wolf, but I know how important it is to have strong, successful males in your corner. If you're a young male and you don't have an older male mentor, seek one out. Ask around in your sports league, your church, and local business groups to see if there is someone with strong ethics, morals, and solid business acumen.

The experience I gained and the education I worked for are the keys that led me to becoming a sports entrepreneur, yet in the beginning I continued to fail as a newcomer to this business because I continued to realize that doing business according to the status quo wasn't for me. I like to say I'm the most successful failure you'll ever meet.

The evolution of the sports industry, because of the stigma, because of the misunderstanding of how the business should be done, has gotten us to this point, and that's why I will highlight in this book where we are, where we could go, and where we probably will go. Fact: the sports industry is changing every day and is going to continue to change and evolve no matter if Michael McGinnis is at the helm, no matter if it's Joe Blow, no matter if it's all of us collectively. In the midst of change it's my hope that this book can serve as a tipping point in the domino effect that leads us in the right direction, a better direction.

Yes, readers, the winds of change are blowing and we need to set our G.P.S. to the right destination so we're not caught on a back road, wondering where we went wrong.

Introduction

Using G.P.S. to Chart Your Sports Course

GPS stands for Global Positioning System. This system uses real-time, 3-dimensional positioning to identify, calculate and show the direction, position and exact location of objects. Most of us have GPS's on our phones and in our cars so we're ready in a couple of clicks to efficiently drive to our destination. This book is your GPS for navigating the sports system. In our case, G.P.S. will serve as an acronym for *Goals*, *Process*, and *Success*, in that order.

The agent-athlete business is presently moving from sports agent to a business manager/consultant/advisor; someone who handles *all* the aspects of the athlete instead of, "Here, let me find you a team." Rather, it will be, "I'm going to help guide you through sports AND life." God willing, you'll play your sport for 20 years, and if you have a business manager, he should be someone who helps lift you up every step of the way, someone who helps you become a legacy for your family, not merely in the financial freedom arena but in achievement and accomplishments.

For us to get to where we need to be, we need to take the right steps and follow precise practices of empowering athletes to realize the power of their platform. We need to help student-athletes and pro athletes maximize their power, and then apply that power to empower others. That's what this book is about—education and empowerment—and it's the underlying motivation for all I do. I want to educate in the sense of helping you the athlete understand what's at play in the world that you want to play in, and how that world works. I've talked to so many parents and athletes, and it astounds me how ill-informed they are on the process they're about to navigate. They're in desperate need of education to deeply understand what they're getting themselves into. The empowerment piece is knowing how to take what you just learned and ask yourself, "Exactly how do I maximize the opportunity I've been given to the fullest extent?"

There are no guarantees in life, so what are you going to do to empower yourself regardless if the process makes you the next star or the next Joe Schmo no one ever hears about? The uncertainty leads to me showing you just how important it is to educate yourself within the process, which in turn leads to empowerment, which ultimately leads to freedom. Because freedom is truly a mindset. A free individual is one who recognizes that freedom is within their own mind, and can take that freedom and apply it to the world in which they live. Don't you see? If we all can be educated, empowered, and recognize our freedom, we will appreciate the value of each individual we interact with, be it the CEO, the janitor, your wife, your kids, and so on. Every person you meet has value, and every person you meet is significant. I'm not saying we'll live in some utopia...the world is the world, and there is always going to be suffering and sacrifice. The money, the fame; that doesn't really matter in the overall picture. My opinion of how money works is that if you're good at something, you work hard enough at it, and you possess some financial intelligence, the money is going to come. As far as fame goes, you can't really control that either.

☙ ❧

Someone once asked me to describe myself in six words. I paused for a quick moment and then responded, "I guess I would say problem-solver, people-connector, and servant-leader." I thought I was done. I thought I had fully answered the question. The interviewer slyly smiled and reminded me that since my answers were hyphenated words, I only had three descriptions. "Okay," I said with a sigh. "Let's add father, husband, and son." She seemed satisfied. My hope is that you'll find those six self-definitions ingrained throughout the pages of this book, for they describe the very essence of who I am. But, alas, this book isn't about me. It's about you; the one who is passionate about playing sports, the one who is steeped in sports business, and the one who is impacted by the culture of sports. Perhaps you'll identify with some or all of my six words. Perhaps you'll unearth your own six words—whatever your six words are, they must be etched into everything you do within the sports world, and within life. They must define and weave between the lines of your understanding of the world and your place within it.

When you finish the last page of this book I want you to take away a deep understanding of how the current sports process allows a young male or female to possess a passion for a game, go from the high school level to the collegiate level, and hopefully, to the professional level. I want parents to take a journey through the process and learn the ins and outs of the current sports landscape so they can be the best supporting cast to their youth athlete. I want anyone who has a desire to work in the sports industry to understand and utilize some of the best practices that are currently in place, to learn what other dynamics are in play today, how the industry is continually evolving, and what innovation you can employ to lean toward the future, fully equipped, fully educated, fully empowered.

The dictionary defines *empower* as "make (someone) stronger and more confident, especially in controlling their life and claiming their rights." That definition embodies what is contained within these pages, and encapsulates the message I desire to get across to you. I want the truths within these pages to sink into your soul and anchor themselves there as you navigate each section of this book.

I hope as you read this book you experience many ah-ha moments. As authors Chip and Dan Heath express in their epic book, The Power of Moments[1], I expect that you'll have some defining moments of elevation, insight, pride, and connection. In so many ways at this point in history I believe people feel as if they don't have choices; that they have to pretty much choose between a bad or a worse decision. I'm here to tell you that no matter what the circumstances are in your life, whatever your socioeconomic status or background, whatever your family structure, you *do* have choices! I'm speaking into your life that you *can* feel empowered to navigate your choices to create a win-win dynamic for yourself and the individuals you aspire to work with, or on behalf of. With that

---

[1] Chip Heath, Dan Heath, *The Power of Moments: Why Certain Experiences Have Extraordinary Impact* (New York, Simon & Schuster; October 3, 2017).

said, I hope your ah-ha moments reveal the fact that you're mighty, and that you own a lot of power, even when you feel powerless. I want to drive home that we are *all* significant. If we choose to embrace our significance and work toward polishing ourselves up, truly anything and everything we set our sights on to accomplish is right in front of us.

This book is for:

- The five-star recruit.
- The kid who never gets off the bench.
- Anyone who is playing a sport at any level who wants to progress and become better, and to push to the next level of their sport.

No matter where you are in your sports journey, you need to equip yourself with the right information so you can make informed, intelligent decisions.

This book is for:

- Those who are supporting the athlete, be it mom, dad, friends, neighbors, extended family.
- Anyone who's on the journey with these young athletes, trying to help them throughout the process.

I want the supporting cast to realize that you play a crucial role even if you're not shooting the shot, running, or whatever the sport happens to be.

This book is for:

- The industry professionals who work inside the world of sports.
- Professional scouts, coaches, agents, and financial advisors.

Your role is absolutely vital to the success of the athlete and how they navigate within their sport. You need to understand your role and significance, employing your unique philosophies, your own practices. It's also vital that industry professionals adopt a servant-leadership process so we can all accomplish more for the athlete and lead the charge as change-leaders within the sports industry. If we can all strive to get to this servant-leadership process where we put others before ourselves, we'll see that it doesn't mean we don't also receive benefit, but that the benefit will be magnified because we will be impacting the lives of others while impacting our own life. Much more can be done when we think about what we as individuals can do for the collective; through serving others we are individually empowered. Without the servant-leader aspect, it's about, "Give me your money and I will perform a service for you," which is so clinical and impersonal. It's so easy in that case to just say, "Yeah, onto the next promising athlete."

※

Early in my career I was striving to make it as an intern, yet after four and a half years I still wasn't succeeding. I remember talking to a mentor-of-sorts about my lack of success and even though he was speaking very specifically to the sports agency industry, he said, "Michael, it's a war of attrition." What he was basically getting at was, *how you succeed is based on where you decide to quit.* His advice at that time resonated with me greatly. So, now I tell you: if you stay on your path, you'll eventually succeed because it is only a matter of timing, and the difference between success and failure is quitting and continuing. If you want something, if you desire to achieve something, it's only a matter of time as long as you stay on that path.

We see it time and time again, in business, sports, life, you name it. We always think it's the one who's the strongest or the smartest, but no, it's the one who's the most determined and the most focused on their goals, and the one who stays focused on their goal the longest. Maintaining determination and focus over a sustained period of time requires one simple component and that component is: be patient. I feel like a lot of times we want things to work on our schedule, and as a person who's a control freak like myself, I had to learn, and am still learning, that life doesn't bend to me. I have realized that I have to bend to life, and be fluid as I navigate through the sports course. I've learned this component throughout my educational life, my professional life and my personal life. I experienced my first vivid real-life lesson in patience when I was a sophomore in high school.

I was 16 years old and I had always succeeded as an athlete. I was never the best by any means, but I was definitely one of the hardest working individuals on any team for which I played. And so my sophomore year was the first time I was ever cut from any sports team. I'd been trying out and playing on sports teams competitively since fifth grade so when I was cut from the basketball team it was a defining moment because that's when I realized that people can try to stop you from achieving a goal, but in reality the only way you won't achieve a goal is if you decide to stop. I remember feeling appalled that another individual would think it was right to tell me he could deny me where I wanted to go. It lit a fire inside, and I felt empowered, I felt determined; I put in more effort toward school and life, and it seemed like the world changed around me. I felt like people took more interest in me, people listened to me. I was happy with myself.

By failing forward and not accepting someone telling me I wasn't good enough one day, I felt awakened because I realized that I *can* create any opportunity I want and just because I failed yesterday, that doesn't mean I will fail today or tomorrow. Being cut from the basketball team in my sophomore year of high school made me realize that *I'm* in control of my life and *I* determine my fate. Sometimes you have to press the reset button when you're around people who are critical or scrutinizing you because you walk away feeling mentally beat up. In those circumstances you must remember to ask yourself, does what that person is saying define me? No! You must remember who you are so when those arrows come, you know how to deflect them.

As an individual, especially in modern day, we believe that finished products should look clean, polished, and pretty on the outside. That may be true if you're buying a TV or a car; you want a flawless look. But a successful individual who we perceive as "finished" has gone through the fire; they're bloody, they're dented, they're impacted, but they're still there, still whole. We don't see the underbelly of their experience, we see what we see on the outside. As I've gone through this journey, and taken my bumps and lumps and bruises, I'm still whole, I'm still solid. I think that's the reality of it—if you have the expectation that you're going to slide through life or business and succeed, and you're going to instantly be the next Bezos or Gates, instantly successful, an ultra-entrepreneur, that's not reality. It's been said it takes decades to become an overnight success.

Below is an excerpt from a speech given by former president Theodore Roosevelt[2] that I believe applies to our reality of being in the sports "arena."

> It is not the critic who counts; not the man who points out how the strong man stumbles, or where the doer of deeds could have done them better. The credit belongs to the man who is actually in the arena, whose face is marred by dust and sweat and blood; who strives valiantly; who errs, who comes short again and again, because there is no effort without error and shortcoming; but who does actually strive to do the deeds; who knows great enthusiasms, the great devotions; who spends himself in a worthy cause; who at the best knows in the end the triumph of high achievement, and who at the worst, if he fails, at least fails while daring greatly, so that his place shall never be with those cold and timid souls who neither know victory nor defeat.

You're going to come through the process of sports and realize you've taken your lumps and bruises, you've stood strong through it all. That sheer fact speaks volumes to your character. And please be clear, it has nothing to do with what you aspire to *do*. It's *who* you are, what you're about, and what your core being is ingrained with that allows you to succeed.

---

[2] Taken from Theodore Roosevelt's speech, "Citizenship in a Republic" delivered at the Sorbonne in Paris, France on April 23, 1910.

The G.P.S. Guide

◈

As I started to learn the business side of an agent's role, the need to truly be a business advisor and uphold fiduciary duties that an agent of record has on behalf of their client became very clear. I hold myself to an extremely high standard and that's what has helped prepare me for this industry, because there are going to be a lot of failure and undesirable circumstances I'm going to have to endure in terms of the shady and unethical situations that often prevail. Sports agents are faced with a daily choice: Either you're going to give in, or you're going to give up. But there is another option: You can rise above it all! I have no desire to give in or give up, and so by keeping an empowerment culture alive in myself, and with other agents doing the same, we can collectively rise above the status quo and provide top-shelf service to our clients. As the current agent business process evolves into a more efficient engine for the athlete, everyone wins!

I wrote this book as a resource manual that athletes, parents, coaches, agents, and sports professionals can go to for concrete answers. The information this book contains is highly applicable and I know you'll amass many take-aways, and like any other course of study, you'll need to take in the information in chunks. There might be some chapters you want to skim at first then come back to, and others in which you'll want to spend more time digesting the material.

By applying the information you learn in this book, you'll get results.

What I ask is that you read this book with an open mind. There is some information about the sports process that we all need to understand, so we'll take a deep dive into a few facts and figures and then apply them by comparing a variety of sports industries, being reflective of the current process, and open-minded to the solution I propose. By the time you read the last page, my hope is that you'll have your own suggestions to add to the solution.

Throughout this book I'll repeatedly reference "stakeholders." By stakeholders I mean players, parents, schools/colleges, pro sports teams, sports business professionals, and fans.

This book is laid out in three primary parts:

In Part One, GOALS, we'll take a look at the geolocation of where we are right now on the sports map. You'll learn the waypoints within sports as I educate you on the current process and dynamics present in amateur, college, and professional sports, and exactly how it all works. Throughout the pages of this book, really within each chapter, I'll help you understand your market value and how to best apply that value so you can capitalize on every opportunity as you're navigating the process. As we progress through Part One, I'll explain how all stakeholders can glean maximum benefits from learning how to navigate the process, and I'll dissect why the current process is off track.

In Part Two, PROCESS, you'll first learn to recalculate the process in order to redirect toward a culture of empowerment. In the second half of Part Two we arrive at the pivotal point of my "empowered solution" where I provide a detailed definition of how to establish and grow a culture of empowerment so we can reach our destination—maximum opportunities for all stakeholders.

In Part Three, SUCCESS, you'll route your way to success through developing an empowered mindset. I'll discuss exactly what components of mental strength are essential during one's journey through sports and you'll collect some pertinent commentary from leading mental strength industry experts.

At the end of each chapter you'll have a chance to engage even further with the Intersection of Education and Empowerment questions and exercise.

We're ready for our journey! Start your engine!

Part I
GOALS

GOAL ONE Find Your Geolocation
Where Are We Now on the Sports Map?

"Change your opinions, keep to your principles; change your leaves, keep intact your roots."

~Victor Hugo

The G.P.S. Guide

Before you embark on a trip to a new destination, it's common to enter the address into your GPS, especially if you're traveling to unfamiliar territory. The first thing the navigation device does is show you where you currently are. You must know where you are before you know where you're going. The same principle applies to your sports journey.

In this chapter I'll talk about where the current process is, how it operates, and map out the dynamics at play within amateur, college, and professional sports. In other words, as the title of this chapter indicates, I'm going to clearly show you where we are right now on the sports map.

However, before we start surveying where we are, I must first express my frustration about what I've heard repeatedly said over the last five plus years. I insert my thoughts here because what I have to say has everything to do with the current climate in the sports world and also serves as a preamble to the remainder of the book. Here goes: The oft-repeated phrase is, "Agents over promise and under deliver." Sports agents should not come in to sell you on what they can do for you yet that's most often foremost on their agenda.

You may be thinking, *Isn't it their job to sell me*? No! It's their job to *market* you to interested parties. As an agent, I should never meet a family and a player to sell MYSELF to them. I should meet a family and a player to *LEARN* about them, to learn about where they want to go, and then educate and empower them along the way. An agent shouldn't be overly involved and he shouldn't be the one directing the show. The agent should be the one who walks lock-step with his client; he should act as the glue for all the other business partners in the process.

Most agents go in and talk about what they've done to help another athlete and his family when his goal should be to market that athlete sitting in front of him to a team and a brand. And I don't mean market in the sense that their client is a commodity, but let's be honest, it's entertainment. It's a business. It's all about who wants whom and for what price. So, if an agent comes knocking at your door and is not even willing to have a conversation about his intentions, then that agent isn't in the right industry. The primary stigma attached to sports agents is that they have greedy, dishonest intentions. I'm well aware that it's difficult to be a good guy in this industry but I'm viewing this problem as an opportunity to create positive change.

Athletes should realize that the platform they have is so much larger and grander than sports, than putting a ball through a hoop, or throwing a football or baseball. An agent's role is really a platform to show individuals that if they want to achieve something, they can, but it takes doing X, Y and Z. An athlete has to understand that this is a business first, and always.

Where are we on the Map?

Our immediate goal now is to step into the world of how the current process works and what an athlete can expect going into the process. It begins with a young athlete having an interest in a sport, playing first on a Pee Wee team, Little League or Pop Warner, and then moving to a competitive level where they're playing with a travel ball team, AAU team, or other select teams where they actually try out for a specific team. This is the infancy stage of the process. Let's take a quick survey of the different sports leagues and teams:

1. **Pee Wee & Pop Warner**: Pop Warner was founded in 1929, and serves as the only youth football, cheerleading & dance organization that requires its participants to maintain academic standards in order to participate. Pee Wee football starts a child playing the game as young as age five and extends to age twelve. Pop Warner's commitment to academics is what separates the program from other youth sports around the world.

2. **Little League:** Although the roots go as far back as the 18th century, official Little League Baseball was founded by Carl Stotz in 1939. Mr. Stotz, George Bebble and Bert Bebble were the first three managers. The basic goal of Little League remains the same as it was in 1939, to give the children of the world a game that provides fundamental principles (sportsmanship, fair play and teamwork) they can use later in life to become good citizens.

3. **Travel Ball Team**: Travel teams visit different cities to play in leagues at "travel league stops" throughout the country as well as "national championships" that are held in different cities at various times throughout the year. Families are opting out of VA-cations and opting in for what one expert calls "TOURNI-cations" where a family pays for all expenses for their youth athlete to play in a tournament somewhere out of town.

According to sports.vice.com[1] "Every summer, thousands of teenage baseball players travel to amateur showcases and tournaments in hopes of being seen by coaches and scouts. In many cases, they pay hefty registration fees for this privilege. They—and their parents—assume that money is well spent, especially if they come from parts of the country that are not traditional hotbeds of baseball talent." The author continues, "Then there are the tournaments, which are separate from the showcases and require joining a travel team—itself a costly proposition. Even watching isn't free: Showcases charge subscription fees for scouts to have access to the reports and full rankings lists. Everyone pays into the machine."

I must add here that travel teams for kids under ten years old are common in the youth sports world because it's perceived that if your kid isn't "performing" by a certain age, he has missed the boat. Larry Owens, Head Baseball Coach for Bellarmine University, had this to say in his opinion article[2]: "In the travel team's defense, it is a lot to ask of a ten-year-old and his family to practice two or three times a week and then play the demanding weekend schedule that can be four or more games in two days. Here lies the problem. The main focus continues to be on the number of games they play, winning tournaments and comparing one kid's ability to others. The focus should be on player and personal development. The need to play on these teams to get opportunities down the road is simply not true at such a young age."

---

1 Wyllys, Jared. "Imperfect Game: Inside the Amateur Baseball Industrial Complex." https://sports.vice.com/en_ca/article/43dggm/imperfect-game-inside-the-amateur-baseball-industrial-complex (accessed 8/23/2018).
2 Owens, Larry. "Travel Baseball-A Flawed System?" https://insidepitchonline.com/travel-baseball-a-flawed-system/ (accessed 8/23/2018).

This astute coach had other bits of wisdom sprinkled throughout his concise article: "Our children's growth from a baseball perspective is being stunted because the system puts too much emphasis on winning tournaments when they are nine years old. This would be my option to travel baseball: Youth Developmental Instructional Leagues." Sage advice from one who has been in the trenches.

I ask you, whatever happened to playing sports for the joy of the game and the lessons team sports affords, rather than focusing so much on winning or losing?

4. **AAU**: Amateur Athletic Union basketball, better known as AAU basketball, is an amateur and youth sports organization, founded in 1888, in Chicago, by a man named William Buckingham Curtis, who wanted to standardize amateur and youth sports. It was originally designed to prepare America's amateur athletes to compete in the Olympics and other prominent international competitions. According to its mission statement, the goal of the AAU is "To offer amateur sports programs through a volunteer base for all people to have the physical, mental, and moral development of amateur athletes and to promote good sportsmanship and good citizenship." The AAU season is typically between the months of March and June, and athletes are assigned to their teams by early February. Most AAU games take place as part of tournaments that are held on the weekends all across the country. How much you travel is essentially based on your team and its schedule, each team varies greatly, but suffice it to say that plenty of travel is a regular part of playing on an AAU team.

Michael McGinnis J.D.

൙   ൞

As a youth is navigating through the beginning process, what the youth and their parents find out is that eventually just going to practice and playing games isn't enough. To reach a higher rung and create more opportunities for themselves, amateur student-athletes and their parents need to look for development opportunities. And that development needs to be physical, mental, and potentially spiritual, depending on the individual.

On the physical side it would be obtaining trainers and coaches to work outside of playing in the games and going to practices. The mental side would be making sure the youth employs mindfulness practices that include journaling, meditation practices, and speaking with mental health coaches and a sport psychologist to make sure they understand how to sharpen their minds to succeed in their respective sport.

There's one thing that may not be applicable to everyone, and I'm not trying to force anything down anyone's throat by any means, but I think another pillar would be the spiritual aspect. Whatever religion or ideology you possess, being spiritually grounded provides a level of clarity, a guide so to speak that whatever you're doing, you realize it's not just for the act of the sport. The spiritual aspect lets you realize that this is merely a platform for you to achieve whatever it is that you desire, and shows you that the sport is just you getting to do something you love and have a passion for, but with that love and passion you're then able to help solve the problem of homelessness, domestic violence, clean water across the world, renewable energy, or whatever your global cause happens to be.

I hate to burst your bubble after talking about spiritual aspects but before we move on to Goal Two, we need to pause our navigation so we can take a stark look at the condition of college basketball as it stands today. We know that the profit sports (football and basketball) are under fire these days but college basketball has taken big hits as of this writing, and the following demonstrates the blatant reality of where we are when it comes to college sports.

On April 25, 2018 the Commission on College Basketball presented their recommendations on how to promote change in college basketball. The commission was created after an FBI investigation resulted in the arrests of ten individuals, including four assistant coaches. A Washington Post[3] article cited on the day the report was released, "It's imperative to remember that the commission's recommendations are just that: recommendations of an independent group. When and how any rule changes will be adopted or implemented is up to the NCAA member schools."

Led by former Secretary of State Dr. Condoleezza Rice, the commission provided its recommendations on several key issues after seeking advice from stakeholders such as players, coaches, administrators, agents, the NBA, and apparel companies. Here are some of the proposed changes:

---

[3]Wallace, Ava. "Breaking down the NCAA basketball report: The key word is 'recommendations'"https://www.washingtonpost.com/news/sports/wp/2018/04/25/breaking-down-the-ncaa-basketball-report-the-key-word-is-recommendations/?noredirect=on&utm_term=.84c40449879c (Accessed 8/29/2018).

1. Recommend to the NBA to get rid of the one-and-done rule by allowing players to enter the draft straight out of high school. In 2006, the NBA and NBPA changed the draft eligibility rule, stating that American players had to be nineteen years old and one year out of high school to enter the draft. The intent of the rule, at the time, was to get NBA personnel out of high school gyms.
2. Allow players who aren't selected in the NBA draft to return to college.
3. Allow NCAA-certified agents to engage with student-athletes in high school, at a certain age or grade (not yet determined). No athlete would lose eligibility by meeting or contacting certified agents.
4. Continue to require players to sit out upon transferring.
5. Strengthen enforcement by creating independent parties to investigate and adjudicate major, complex cases.
6. Increase the penalty structure for a Level I violation and make it unyielding, such as a multi-season ban.
7. Enact a new summer basketball model, with the help of the NBA, NBPA and USA basketball.
8. Apparel companies would cooperate in helping clean up summer basketball.
9. Change the Board of Governors structure with at least five independent voices as part of the governing body.

10. Schools can no longer defend a fraud case or misconduct on the basis that "all students, not just athletes, were permitted to benefit" from that fraud.

Although the commission withheld on debating whether college athletes should be compensated for their likeness due to continued litigation, it did state in the deep belly of the report, "paying modest salaries to Division I basketball players will not address the particular corruption the Commission confronts, nor will providing student-athletes a modest post-graduation trust fund based on licensing of names, images and likeness."

That's an interesting finding because former Northwestern quarterback Kain Colter, co-founder of the College Athletes Players Association (CAPA), said publicly, "The current model resembles a dictatorship, where the NCAA places these rules and regulations on these students without their input or without their negotiation."

According to a Sports Illustrated article[4], "In 2012, Colter worked on a study with Drexel professor Ellen Staurowsky that found that the average scholarship fell short of what top-division football players needed by more than $3,000 a year, while more than 80% of athletes playing football on "full scholarship" lived below the poverty line. What's more, the study found that if revenues were shared among players and owners as in pro sports, each Division I football player would be worth $137,357 per year."

---

4 Nocera, Joe, Ben Strauss, "Fate of the Union: How Northwestern football union nearly came to be" https://www.si.com/college-football/2016/02/24/northwestern-union-case-book-indentured (Accessed 8/29/2018).

What? Unionize?

Another warning light to the status quo of where we are now on the sports map is unionization by players. Through the years there have been attempts to unionize college athletes, raising questions about the extent to which college athletes are employees. The ongoing debate of the unionizing of players is a hot topic among government, education, and student-athlete rights advocates.

One Forbes article[5] states, "National Labor Relations Board's regional director in Chicago ruled that members of Northwestern University's football team were eligible to vote for union representation if they wanted. The key to that ruling was the regional director's opinion that college football players are "employees" within the meaning of the National Labor Relations Act and therefore eligible to unionize."

The final result was predictable. Findlaw.com[6] reports, "Football players at Northwestern University recently sought classification as employees entitled to certain rights and obligations in a bid to organize a union. The National Labor Relations Board (NLRB), the federal organization responsible for organizing labor unions, unanimously declined to classify the student athletes as employees."

I could fill volumes of books with legal rhetoric regarding the on again off again status of the student-athlete and where

---

5 Leef, George, "Federal Official Again Declares That College Football Players Can Unionize" https://www.forbes.com/sites/georgeleef/2017/02/22/federal-official-again-declares-that-college-football-players-can-unionize/#675227df42e7 (Accessed 8/29/2018).
6 FindLaw.com, "Can College Athletes Unionize?" https://education.findlaw.com/higher-education/can-college-athletes-unionize.html (Accessed 8/29/2018).

he stands in relation to the NCAA (National Collegiate Athletic Association), NCSA (Next College Student Athlete), CAPA (College Athletes Players Association), and the host of other organizations. Suffice it to say that knowledge is power, education holds the key to empowerment for all stakeholders.

I've covered some heavy topics in Goal One so it's time to lighten things up a bit and turn our attention to learning the waypoints on how to navigate the current process now that you have a concrete understanding of what the current process is and how it operates. However, before we move ahead, let's first pause to answer the Direction Questions and then peer into the first Q & A session to see what coach Ron Slusher has to say. His seasoned wise words will surely illuminate the way forward.

Intersection of Education and Empowerment

Direction Questions:

Where are you currently on the conveyor belt? Youth league? AAU? Amateur league? Traveling league? University level? Going into or at the pro level?

If you plan on moving to the next level of play, what is your daily action plan for getting there?

Empowerment Exercise:

Take a moment and assess your goals, objectives, and desired end result. Think about what values and character traits you want to anchor in your heart and soul through your sports journey. Who will you become throughout your journey?

Q & A Session

Ron Slusher
President and Manager, Ohio Warhawks

Q: Share a little bit about your background as a coach.

A: I coached high school basketball, high school baseball, football, track, for about fifteen years. I've been a coach with the Ohio Warhawks for…let's just say about thirty-five years. I was an associate scout with the Cincinnati Reds for twenty-five years and for the past five years I've scouted for the Atlanta Braves.

Q: What aspects do you like about coaching?

A: When you work with young men you always like to be in a situation where you can help these young guys develop their talent on the field and develop their minds and learn to take responsibility for their actions. We've been doing this with the Warhawks for thirty plus years! These young athletes come to Springfield, Ohio, stay for the summer, and that's where they learn all these good habits.

Q: How do you incorporate teaching your athletes values and character combined with training them in the physical aspects of the game?

A: Well, first of all they have to understand they're away from mommy, daddy, girlfriend; everything is not handed to them, they learn that wake-up calls are at eight o'clock in the morning. You've got to get up on your own, and of course we make sure they have access to transportation to and from all their workouts and other related activities. It's vital that they develop habits of doing things the right way and they have to take on a lot of responsibility at this level to help prepare them for the next level of college and/or pro baseball. They soon realize they just can't come in here and act like spoiled kids as many of them are accustomed to at home.

Q: How important do you think it is for parents to educate themselves and their student-athlete in the process of succeeding in sports?

A: I think it's very important that they educate themselves but not just about athletics. Parents need to realize that their kids are not going to be living with them the rest of their lives so they have to educate them on everything; responsibility, respect, how to prepare themselves to be successful away from home. It's often difficult for parents to adjust to their child growing up because they always want to control their kids. Sometimes kids have to make up their own minds on what they want to do. Parents have got to make sure they help prepare their kids for the next level—even if it's teaching their kids how to do their own laundry or taking out the trash or mowing the lawn or cleaning their room, there are things kids need to know in order to make their lives work. The kids who learn how to do basic household and yard tasks tend to be very successful. The truth is: some kids never adjust being away from home because they don't know how to manage themselves on a daily basis.

Q: Is the inability of a young athlete to manage his basic daily duties apparent to you fairly quickly?

A: Yes, it's apparent to me after a few phone calls with mommy and daddy.

Q: How do you deal with it when you see a youth who has a whole bunch of promise as an athlete and yet you know that the parents have really strong apron strings tied to their son?

A: I give them examples. These are very, very talented kids we deal with. Some of these kids are mature and some are not mature, and the parents have to understand one thing, and that is, a) if your son has big talent, he's going to go to college, and all you can do is trust that everything you taught him growing up is going to carry on with him. There are going to be a lot of things out there to distract him and try to sway him away such as partying and drugs, peer pressure and girls. This is what I tell parents: you can keep him home as long as you want, but there's going to come a time where he's got to go to college, and if he's lucky enough to get drafted out of high school, and if the money is enough for him to sign a league contract and take him away from college, he had better be prepared. Because he's going to be put in situations that he's never been put in before. He's going to be away from home for a long time. And sometimes pro teams put two or three kids in dorms and they're not supervised. The major league team doesn't care what they do because they're assuming the kid has already learned to be responsible and knows how to handle things. When it comes to a seventeen-year-old kid out of high school who just signed a five-million-dollar contract, you're trying to tell me that that kid is ready for what's about to be thrown at him? Some of the young athletes from other countries like to party; they're accustomed to staying out until two, three o'clock in the morning, and then going to practice at six o'clock in the morning. All of a sudden your bouncing baby boy is staying in the same room with a couple of these guys and now they're thinking they can try that lifestyle too. No. No. No. No. The only thing you can do is hope your son is mature enough to say, "Hey man, I appreciate it but that's not for me." I've had a couple kids in the past who have played for me and yielding to peer pressure didn't go their way.

One of my athletes was a very sheltered kid from Maryland. He was a top draft pick and got drafted by the Atlanta Braves. I think it was 2003 or 2004, and he fell asleep at a red light after partying all night and the police found him drunk at the steering wheel. The Braves got rid of him and then he went on to Washington. The kid bounced around and got hooked on drugs and alcohol and his life spiraled out of control. These kids don't wake up one day and say, "Hey, I'm going to have me a beer and start doing drugs." No, they've been doing that crap at home. They've been doing this while their mom and dad go out on the weekends and party. The parents leave their kids all alone and their buddies come over and they go out and go to wild parties and stay out all night with friends. When a young athlete comes to the Warhawks and then messes up in some way, I give them a second chance because everybody deserves a second chance. When I do give a kid a second chance and he does something stupid after that, well there's no tolerance at that point. You're gone. Because whenever kids come up here to Ohio, you put your faith in the Ohio

Warhawks to make sure the kids are supervised, which they are. I've sent first-round draft picks home and no-round draft picks home because of drinking, drugs, smoking cigarettes, and just doing stupid stuff. If I'm going to recruit your son to come up here, you don't want to hear that the Ohio Warhawks let kids get away with stuff.

As soon as young athletes hit the college scene, a lot of parents accept the stuff that's there; they think *oh well I was a kid one time, and that's what I did*. Well that doesn't make it right. Most young people are not prepared for the temptations that await them at college. And I don't care if it's Brigham Young University, I don't care if it's Ohio State, I don't care if it's Cedarville Christian College, there are kids on every campus who engage in dangerous activities. It happens every day.

Q: How do you recognize leadership in an athlete when they first come to you?

A: Leadership comes in different shapes, sizes, and angles. Leadership can be vocal or quiet, but a true leader leads by example. A leader is a great team player by working harder than anyone else. He gets along with his teammates, he doesn't try to impress people. Leadership can also come from a really cocky kid, kind of a smartass sometimes, but on the flipside, he demands respect from his teammates by the way he acts on the practice field, the weight room, around the Hawks nest (where the kids stay with us in the summertime).

The first two or three days of the kids coming into our program, I tell them, "Okay, listen, how many of you guys are three-hole hitters on your team?" Almost half the team raises their hand, and that tells me that these guys are talented, because if they're hitting a three-hole, that's one of the best places to hit in the batting order. Then I ask them, "How many of you guys were high school captains of your high school team?" Bam, ninety-eight percent of the hands always pop up. They're leaders. And the other kids who don't raise their hands are the kids who are usually the underclassmen and they just haven't had their chance yet. There are some kids that you can just see leadership in their eyes, in the way they act. Those are the guys I want! I want the guys who will go through a wall for you, they're up in the morning, they're doing their job, their chores, they go out to the batting cages and they do things on their own to better themselves. They go out and run a mile on their own. They don't need mommy or daddy to hold their hand. They're doing these things because they know what they're supposed to do. Those are the kids who are typically going to make it in life beyond baseball because they have a goal and they know what they're trying to do.

Sometimes it takes us a while to weed out the bad kids, but once we do, we send them home. We don't tolerate nonsense. We don't charge these kids a penny to play, and if I'm going to pay for everything, by God they're going to do things in the right way or I'm not going to waste my time. If they're not coachable, their young asses are gone. And one thing I've noticed—things have changed over the years. The kids these days are not as tough as they used to be. They're real soft. And that comes from mommy and daddy. Everything is handed to them, they don't have to work for anything. Conversely, a lot of kids we get are not from rich families and these are the kids who work at McDonald's on the side; they've learned to make some extra money to help mom and dad out. Those are the kids I want. I want those kids who want to work.

The kids who haven't had anything handed to them are the kids who understand at an early age that they've got to work for everything they get. They're usually the hardest working kids on my team. I get kids from California who call their parents by their first name. I get kids from the South and it's, "Yes sir, no sir, and thank you." I'll ask the kids from the South in front of the other kids, "What would happen if you called your mom and dad by their first name?" Without hesitation, they say, "My dad would knock me out." They've learned respect at a young age.

One of the biggest compliments we get is usually from the mothers after their kids go back home. We'll get a call from mom and it goes something like this: "Coach Slusher, who is this guy taking out my trash? Who is this guy who is now making his bed? Who is this guy who is now doing his own laundry? Who is this guy who's mowing the grass, doing things to help out?" I say, "Well, that's the same kid you always had but you never made him do those things." I just tell them how it is.

Q: What is a frustration or challenge that you've experienced as a coach?

A: I don't see any frustration. That is, once you lay down the ground rules from the get-go. When I talk to parents on the phone, I introduce myself and explain, "Your son is not going to play every inning, nothing is going to be handed to him, he's going to be treated just like everybody else, he's got to get used to being away from home because when he goes to college, he's going to need to be prepared." Since we get kids from fourteen years old to nineteen years old, we start as soon as they arrive, to teach manners, ethics, and skills. Some of these kids though just don't have what it takes to thrive in a team living environment.

I remember I had this kid once come from out of state, very late in the season, a first-round draft pick. He walked in the Nest, which is basically a dorm. There are a lot of young men sleeping in there so the place is going to be a little dirty. In all honesty, I don't care what the Nest looks like, as long as the guys don't destroy stuff and waste food. I don't care how it looks at twelve o'clock but come nine o'clock before they go to bed, that place better be immaculate clean. Well, this kid called me and told me he had just arrived and I was maybe five minutes away. Before I arrived the kid walked in the Nest to see what it was like. I get there and ask, "Where's the new kid?" One of the other kids said, "He just walked in and walked out. He went home." I called the kid up and asked, "Where are you?" He said, "Oh coach, I don't think it's going to work out." I told him, "Listen, this is a dorm for boys and coaches. We're all buddies here, we can let our hair hang down, but the Nest has got to be cleaned up one time a day. Son, if you're that picky, you may not want to go to college. You just better stay home and let mommy and daddy take care of you." I laughed and wished him good luck and he went on and he played pro ball for about eight years.

Q: What is your best piece of advice for parents who have young athletes coming through the system?

A: Start right now by teaching your kids good habits and responsibility. I see a lot of parents doing everything for their kids. Simple things like staying on top of their school work and getting enough quality sleep—they have to have at least eight hours of sleep in order for them to function as young adults. If parents don't prepare their youngsters, when those kids go off to college all of a sudden they're thrown into the college atmosphere and very often get caught up in partying, drinking, and drugs. A lot of kids come to us not even knowing how to boil an egg. They don't know how to wash their clothes or do much of anything. Parents, teach your kids how to change a flat tire! I've had kids who got a flat tire and they would call me and say, "Coach Slusher I got a flat tire." I would respond with, "Don't you know how to fix it?" More times than not they said, "No." I would ask them, "What would happen if you were back home?" to which they'd reply, "I'd call dad or mom." I always responded with, "Stay right there." I'd drive to where they were and tell them step by step how to change that tire while they performed each step themselves.

There are so many life experiences that you learn when you get out on your own and gain a little freedom. It's all not hunky-dory, everything's not all apple pie and Chevrolet, but there comes a time when a kid has got to grow up and learn to take care of himself, and do things in the right way, and learn from his experiences. I teach the young athletes that come through our program to always be honest and always try to make the right decision, and treat people with respect. The respect factor is probably one of the biggest things I try to teach kids: when you give somebody your word, you do everything you can to live up to that word. Some of these young athletes don't know how to properly treat girls. They treat girls like they're just a rag doll and excuse my language, but they treat them like a piece of meat. Sometimes that doesn't improve with age; in fact it often gets worse. I find out very quickly what kind of character these guys have because I tell them, "When you ride in a Warhawks van to go to the store or go to the weight room, we've got Warhawks written all over our vans and everybody in Springfield knows where we stay."

Coaching baseball is the easy task. Teaching some of these kids who have no home training how to act right and exhibit good character, now that's another story! When we get these kids, we do show a lot of favoritism—I play favoritism with all of them.

GOAL TWO

Learn the Waypoints on How to Navigate the Current Process

"Efforts and courage are not enough without purpose and direction."

~John F. Kennedy

We move onward! We have a ton of information to cover in this chapter so let's get rolling.

After a young athlete plays in Little League, Pop Warner, AAU, or Travel Ball, and increases his developmental skills even further during middle school, the next step would be working up to the high school level. The student-athlete starts to gain a little more exposure and recognition from the collegiate coaches if he follows the proper steps to build himself up physically, mentally, and spiritually at the middle school and high school levels.

As the student-athlete enters the high school level, that's when some universities will start sending letters to show their interest, coaches will come out to see them, and that's when the whole recruiting/scouting process really starts at the collegiate level.

Before we continue, let's take a more in-depth look at the recruiting process.

The bottom line of recruiting: College recruiting is a process by which coaches identify potential recruits, evaluate them, and ultimately decide on the offers they are going to make. Steps involve initial letters, questionnaires, and camp invites, preliminary evaluations by recruiters, followed up by phone calls, visits, social media interaction, and in-person evaluations, and ultimately a verbal offer, and then of course signing the athlete. This is a good time to be realistic about the chances of entering into a college athletic program.

Based on an NCAA report[1] [last updated April 20, 2018], the overall estimated probability for athletes getting from high school to playing in an NCAA school in the profit sports are as follows:

Men's Basketball:

High School Participants: 550,305

NCAA Participants: 18,712

Overall Percent HS: 3.4%

% HS to NCAA Division I: 1.0%

% HS to NCAA Division II: 1.0%

% HS to NCAA Division III: 1.4%

Football:

High School Participants: 1,057,382

NCAA Participants: 73,063

Overall Percent HS: 6.9%

% HS to NCAA Division I: 2.7%

% HS to NCAA Division II: 1.8%

% HS to NCAA Division III: 2.4%

---

[1] Sources: High school figures from the 2016-17 High School Athletics Participation Survey conducted by the National Federation of State High School Associations; data from club teams not included. College numbers from the NCAA 2016-17 Sports Sponsorship and Participation Rates Report.

Men's Baseball:

High School Participants: 491,790

NCAA Participants: 34,980

Overall Percent HS: 7.1%

% HS to NCAA Division I: 2.1%

% HS to NCAA Division II: 2.2%

% HS to NCAA Division III: 2.8%

How to Get Recruited for an Athletic Scholarship

Coaches fill scholarship positions based on their program needs so your "job" is to place yourself in a position to receive a scholarship. There are already tried and true methods on how to attract athletic scholarships so don't feel like you have to re-create the wheel.

First, make a long list of schools you'd like to attend, keeping in mind your athletic ability and current academic level; if you struggled all through school, chances are you won't want to place yourself at risk in a highly stringent academic environment. Don't worry, you will narrow your list as you go. Once you've compiled your school list, then create a spreadsheet for the contact information for all the coaches of those schools. You'll need email addresses and phone numbers.

When your information is complete, create a resume or one-sheet infographic showing the seasons you've played your sport, and double- and triple-check all your facts and stats so there are no discrepancies. Be sure to include a copy of your high school transcripts and test scores. Initiate conversations with the coaches on your list and respond quickly when they email you. Double-check your spelling and grammar so you put your best foot forward.

Do some research on the school so you can ask intelligent questions of the coach; make it your business to know what kind of season his team had last year, and be ready to explain why you're interested in that particular school.

Once you've completed the above steps, it's time to attend summer camps and showcases where you can gain exposure and possibly be "discovered" although you shouldn't rely on this as the end-all be-all of the process. Showcases work if a coach is there to watch you because you've reached out to him previously. As with everything else, make sure you send a follow-up email thanking the coach for watching you, and asking about the next step in his recruiting process. Show your respect and gratitude by thanking the referees, scorekeepers, your teammates and the opposing team. How you interact with others will be reflected in how others perceive and interact with you. Yes, it's possible to be competitive AND at the same time be courteous, caring and considerate.

If you are serious about entering the world of college athletics, you will need to study up on the NCAA and NAIA rules and regulations. Read their guides for college bound student-athletes so you know proper protocol for communication between you and coaches. At this point it's time to register with the NCAA and NAIA Eligibility Centers so you're cleared to receive academic scholarships. Determine your core classes and grade/exam requirements so you remain academically eligible. Once you know the requirements, you can organize your academic calendar accordingly. And, remember: schools are not recruiting your parents, they're recruiting you, so be actively engaged throughout the process. You're fortunate if your parents and coaches want to be involved in helping you make informed decisions, but you must be willing to put in some sweat equity yourself.

In addition to the points I just listed, I've included below a few simple proactive steps adapted from an NCSA article, *35 Steps All Athletes Can Take to Win an Athletic Scholarship*,[2] that will help put you ahead of the pack for a college scholarship.

- If you want to be taken seriously, this is not the time for selfies in your bathroom mirror. An appropriate photo on your scouting report will go a long way in letting coaches know you mean business.

- Make sure you have a professional-sounding voicemail. Recruiters should not hear "Yo, hit me back up" when they hear your message, nor should they hear several minutes of your favorite rap song. Record a business-like but friendly message that invites them to leave a voicemail.

- Likewise, provide coaches with a professional email to communicate with you. Email addresses like 2hot4u@anyemail will not make a good first impression. Select an email that exudes professionalism.

---

[2] NCSA. https://www.fastweb.com/student-news/articles/the-35-steps-all-athletes-can-take-to-win-an-athletic-scholarship, 2011, (Accessed 8/28/2018).

- Coaches want to see varsity level game film because it helps them evaluate your playing/position style. Put some clips together of your best plays that are readily available.

- When coaches talk to you or ask you questions, this is your chance to wow them with your personality so don't respond with one-word answers.

- It's best practice not to cold call coaches. Email them your information before you call so they know a little about who you are. Include your full name in the subject line so you're easy to look up.

- This is not just about a school being interested in you. You must do your research to see if the school is a good fit for you. Consider school size, location and distance from home, day-to-day cost of living, majors offered, academic requirements, student population. When you visit schools, trust your gut. If something just doesn't feel right, rely on your instinct.

- When you talk to a coach on the phone, suggest that you visit the school. Don't wait for him to offer. Always contact the coach first, and get confirmation that he knows you're coming.

- Be proactive in asking coaches exactly what their recruiting timeline is so you can plan accordingly.

- Watch what you post on social media. Images and words travel fast in the cyber world and you don't want to sully your reputation and image with unfavorable posts.

- When it comes to coaches, don't be afraid of asking where and how you will fit into the team. You can't automatically assume you're going to start as a freshman. Ask him how you stack up on his recruiting list.

- Here's a tip from thebestschools.org : "Face it, some players will get offers early because of their athleticism, size, or talent. Some young athletes simply have amazing gifts beyond compare. Making that your concern may hamper or derail your own progress. Be inspired, rather than discouraged, by the success of others. Let it push you to strive for improvement."

When you are nearing the end of your high school years is the time when you'll need to go through the NCAA Clearinghouse[3], and at that point you should start figuring out what you have an interest in studying at the next level, and what geographic areas you'd like to explore. It's important to keep in mind that only about two percent of high school athletes are awarded university athletics scholarships and even fewer become professional athletes. Why do I say that at this point when I'm talking about recruiting and scholarships? Because it's crucial to be realistic through the process; the saying *always have a Plan B* is no truer than in college and professional sports.

By the time you reach the high school level, and are seriously considering what college you want to play at, you should really be homed in on *who* you want to become through

---

[3] According to athleticscholarships.net, "There are two situations where you need to register with the NCAA Clearinghouse (now called the Eligibility Center). If a college coach asks you to register or requests your NCAA ID number, you need to create your account. The second situation is, if you are in your junior year and you are sure you are getting recruited by an NCAA DI or DII program.

the process, not just your athletic skills. Why? Because as you transition from Little League level to high school level to college level, it is undeniable that the conveyor belt process has begun. The "conveyor belt" is a term William Rhoden, New York Times sports columnist, uses throughout his historic book, *Forty Million Dollar Slaves: The Rise, Fall, and Redemption of the Black Athlete*[4], to describe the state of black athletes in America. I must interject here that the current conveyor belt system applies to *all* young athletes, no matter what race, and unless you're informed and educate yourself on the process, plan to strap yourself to the conveyor belt and go along for the ride. The conveyor belt continues to move no matter what the athlete thinks or wants to do; the minute he starts receiving recognition from collegiate coaches and schools, the student-athlete is then put into a database or process where he is being tracked and monitored, be it social media, or in person at games, so he needs to be continually mindful at that point of his brand and image. By this point he needs to know exactly what he wants from the process, and he needs to recognize what is important for him as a person as he's making these decisions.

As you, the student-athlete, advance through the process, you'll need to refine your personal values even more, because you'll soon need to make a decision based on the terms of offers that will undoubtedly start coming your way—and those offers can come in as early as your first year in high school all the way to your senior year in high school.

When the offers come in from colleges, you'll determine the amount of scholarships you'll need to attend a particular

---

[4] Rhoden, William C., Forty Million Dollar Slaves: The Rise, Fall, and Redemption of the Black Athlete, New York, Three Rivers Press, 2006.

school, if the colleges meet the criteria you have in place, and if they fit into how you plan on selecting a university. Will you alone decide? Will your parents help you decide? Will you go to mentors, coaches, or a specific teacher that you know will give you wise counsel? You should have a trusted support process around you; those who know you well, who educate themselves on how the recruitment process works in terms of what you can and cannot do, and what those who are recruiting you can and cannot do.

According to ncaa.org, "Full scholarships cover tuition and fees, room, board and course-related books. Most student-athletes who receive athletics scholarships receive an amount covering a portion of these costs." Do your research and encourage your support team to do their research so you can avoid any undue burdens during the recruitment process. Remember, it's not just about the university wanting you to play for them, it's about whether the university's culture is a good fit for you too!

Okay, now you've made your selection, and you've either decided to go off to your respective school, or not. In the baseball realm, after you reach the maturation of a senior in high school, there is the potential to go out for the MLB draft although most high school players are not ready; most need to mature. It comes down to what characteristics you want in a potential offer, and what you think you can provide a franchise. The steps are the same for a student-athlete preparing for the MLB draft, or going off to college basketball, football, you name it.

And so at this point, that's where you need to make sure you understand the eligibility requirements, what it takes to stay at that school, what the school requires of you in terms of the service you'll provide the school as a student-athlete, the time commitment, and how to balance your athletic life and your "real" life.

It will be important for you to use the university's support process. You'll need the people who helped you get to the college level to make sure you're navigating the process successfully, not merely as a passenger, but understanding the implications of signing the NLI to play for a Division I or II school, and what comes along with your commitment to the school, and the school's commitment to you. Resourcefulness will be your BFF because you'll need it to learn how to best tap into every resource at your disposal so you won't just perform as an average-Joe student or student-athlete, but thrive and succeed. The opportunity to play college athletics and receive a scholarship is a privilege, and it is one that comes with, for lack of a better term, strings attached. It's imperative that you recognize what those strings are made of so they don't pull you in a direction you don't aspire to go.

In case you're not familiar with what is needed for a Division I, II, or III school, or if you're still undecided, here's a quick primer according the ncaa.org[5] website:

Division I or II

You need to be certified by the NCAA Eligibility Center to compete at an NCAA Division I or II school. Create a

---

[5] https://web3.ncaa.org/ecwr3/

Certification Account and we'll guide you through the process. You need to create a Certification Account to make official visits to Divisions I and II schools or to sign a National Letter of Intent.

Division III or Undecided

Create a Profile Page if you plan to compete at a Division III school or are not yet sure where you want to compete.

You'll get an NCAA ID, and we will send you important reminders as you complete high school.

Movin' on Up…

You're now a collegiate athlete going through the same process as you were in high school. You're separating from the past, and you're focusing on your mental, physical and spiritual development that will take you into your future. You're going to start receiving interest from professional scouts, teams and organizations. And don't forget the barrage of financial advisors and agents that will descend on you, depending on how marketable or how good of a return on an investment you appear to be.

At the collegiate level, it's even more important that the process and preparation of what you want to achieve align with the intentions of the individuals who aspire to do business with you at the professional level. The process involves consulting your support network, tapping into all the resources you have at the collegiate level, and ensuring that you educate yourself for alignment with NCAA practices, as well as the practices of your specific sports league to ensure you do not violate any of the rules.

And through that process, you'll then make the determination on who you would like to work with you in a professional capacity, be it an advisor, an agent, or what have you. Make your educated and calculated decision within the established regulations, and with the right opportunities you'll expectantly embark on your journey to play at the professional level. Keep in mind though that there is still a lot of uncertainty—no matter how talented you are, there are no guarantees. Playing at the professional level isn't the end-all be-all in realizing that you need to see the bigger picture: you've used the process to create opportunities for yourself, yet those opportunities can change over time. You're also dependent on marketing your skill set so it's imperative that you continually prepare for varying opportunities and continuously educate yourself on understanding your market value and how to raise that value. If the stars align, events work out in your favor, and you get the recognition you need from the pro teams and leagues, you will then gain your opportunity to have your name called and enter the professional ranks.

Now that I've touched on what it takes to rise up to getting pro attention, let's dive a bit deeper into the collegiate level pool. I get the following question a lot and I want to address it here: Should a student-athlete sign the NLI? It's a longstanding debate but I'll give you some of my insight and wisdom regarding how to navigate the waters of the NLI.

A young athlete should hold off as long as possible before signing the NLI or making any form of commitment.

First and foremost, the earlier you commit, the more you limit your opportunities. If you commit as a freshman when five schools are looking at you, you're not able to see the fact that there could be 20 schools looking at you as a senior.

Now granted, there is some risk associated with not signing an NLI, but I think you have to have faith in yourself, trust the process, and realize that your goal is to make a decision based *on* opportunity, and not a decision based on your *lack* of opportunity. So being patient and holding off on signing the NLI until the tail end of your high school career is the best course of action for the athlete.

Often, the fear factor takes over. You believe you won't get any better offers than the one you get in your freshman or sophomore year but I'm here to tell you, if you have the talent and ethics to make it as a top athlete coming into high school, there WILL be other offers.

Don't make a decision based on fear. Make a decision because you *do* want to do it. I hear all the time from high school players who say, "I'm just done with it, I want to select this or that draft advisor. I want to select this or that school."

When I was in law school I heard an oft-repeated phrase that I loved: "You don't know what you don't know." I know all you can do is make a decision with the facts you have today, but I think patience is a great virtue when, if you're talented, you're going to get your opportunity, it is going to come, and you just have to believe that. I'm not talking blind hope here. You'll have indicators. If you're a five-foot center, and you're a senior in high school and you think you're going to the NBA, that's probably not realistic, but again, that doesn't mean you should make a decision based on those circumstances. You should make a decision based on where you want to go, and work backwards.

You'll know if you're being sought after because agents and coaches will make their presence known. If you're not being sought after, there are always recruitment services like National College Scouting Association (NCSA). Again, going back to the five-foot center who has aspirations to go into the NBA, scouting services can create opportunities for an athlete who maybe would not have gotten in through the traditional route because they didn't pass what is referred to as "the look" test. It all comes down to educating yourself so you can use all the resources out there. Self-education should be at the top of your priority list.

Based on what's currently happening with the FBI investigation into college basketball and the concussion issues in the NFL, the sports industry will be dramatically different over the next decade. Parents, if you have a two-year-old who you know will want to play soccer in a couple of years, or you have a senior who's on his way to college, it's crucial that you stay current and informed on what is happening in the industry, both in the news and legal issues. Your education should consist of researching the institutions you aspire to do business with, researching the individuals you aspire to do business with, and making sure you understand the rules and regulations for each entity. Agents, lawyers and financial people are great, but you should not hand over all your power to them…you need to be the one steering the ship. No matter what your economic level, parents need to stay informed about their student-athlete and who's approaching them, and who has their best interest in mind. Do your homework!

Some parents, or a single mother, could consider their student-athlete their meal ticket out of poverty, out of underprivileged, underserved neighborhoods. Often, parents in these communities don't read the fine print let alone the large print of what the finely-dressed, smooth-talking, smiling faces coming to them are offering. So she just pushes her child along. Maybe it's a two-parent underserved home but both parents are working two and three jobs to survive and are simply trusting whoever is knocking on their door, selling the snake oil of a lucrative sports career.

I'm not saying this is true in every case because it certainly isn't; sometimes it's legit. There are honest, ethical agents and coaches out there who do have your child's best sports interests in mind. I'm going to keep stressing this throughout this book but the education part of the sports equation cannot be overstated.

In Southern California with a multitude of affluent families, money isn't the issue. Most of the time it's the parents and student-athlete not having a clear understanding of what they truly want. The sizzle or wow factor of monetary gain might not exist in more affluent homes yet the draw comes in when parents want their student-athlete represented by a big name they believe will make their youth a household name; they want prestige, media, and all the trappings. Even affluent parents don't seem to understand that what your mission is needs to be identified, and if you say, "Oh we just want to get drafted high," well, what does that mean to your student-athlete and to you as parents?

Every parent in every community, before day one of your youth playing any type of sport, ask yourselves two questions: 1) What is your purpose? 2) What is your mission? When you educate yourself internally on what you and your student-athlete are all about, then you'll be able to decipher the BS from what really aligns with your mission.

As a student-athlete, you might tell me, "I've already drafted high. I'm good." Well what does that mean? Does that mean you want to be drafted high for ego's sake? There's nothing wrong with that if that's your mission. Or, does it mean that you feel it will give you the best opportunity to stay around in the sport the longest? Or, do you want to go with the teams that have the higher picks because they're in your region? Or, do you want the security of being a higher pick? A lot of times student-athletes allow what they see on TV and read about mega sports stars to dictate what they want to do.

Don't look at LeBron James and where he is today and mentor yourself on how you become LeBron James because that's how you'll navigate. Look back 18 years when LeBron was just a name in the Ohio area on his way up, trying to go through the collegiate ranks. Yes, you need to look where you want to go, and work backwards, starting from where you are today.

If you want to be the next LeBron James, look at where he started and then navigate from there, instead of saying you want to be LeBron James because you see where he is today. If you go about it from that standpoint you might demand the same status, stardom, and stats. Then when the business side comes in, and you discover that you are nowhere near

King James' current market value, you either give up, pound your chest and holler, or you start at square one like every great athlete. No matter what scouts or agents or schools are telling you, no young athlete has LeBron's market value, simply because you're not in his position. We can all say that LeBron became an overnight success, but it took 18 years. He's been in the league 15 years now. When he started playing professionally, he initiated a meticulous and methodical planning process with his agent and advisors.

Adonal Foyle, retired Warriors player of ten years, continues to have his accountant, business manager, and investment advisors audit each other annually. Checks and balances work because they instill accountability. In his book *The Athlete CEO*[6], Adonal speaks to rookies about how important it is to be the CEO of your empire. In other words, run your athletic career like you would run a business.

Young athletes and their parents often don't anticipate the business side of things. All they see are people coming to their door giving them top-shelf shoes or allowing the family to go see a big-league pitcher throw. All those things are cool, but again, if you don't, from day one, know what your mission, your values, your pillars, and your philosophies are, and know where you want to go, you cannot successfully navigate the journey. Establish your end goals early on because if you don't establish that end goal, what you're really doing is taking your current value of being a successful young amateur athlete and allowing others to tell you what you're going to do, instead of you deciding and charting your course. It's too easy to get knocked off course in the sports world so do the work at the onset. If you don't have a strong, stable family structure, or

---

[6] Foyle, Adonal, *The Athlete CEO* (Realization Press, 2017).

a strong male presence your life, seek out the counsel of a trusted teacher or coach (probably more than one) so you gain a balanced perspective.

At the end of the day sports is a talent-based industry business. It's extremely superficial, and once you demonstrate talent potential at a young age, others are going to try to tell you what *they* want to do with your potential. And just because you can throw a fastball at 105 miles an hour as a senior in high school, maybe your passion isn't to be a big-league pitcher and go to the World Series and be the Cy Young winner. Maybe it's to take your talent to get a free education, or to potentially start your own training process, to start your own training academy.

The bottom line is: If you don't control what you can control in the process, the process will, without a doubt, control you. Just because you're talented enough to play in the MLB, do you want to play 162 baseball games a year? Do you want to have a job where you get a couple months off? Do you want to be under constant scrutiny?

So let's turn a corner here. I've talked about the current process and the process within the process. Now let's excavate the dynamics within the amateur, college, and professional process.

The overall key dynamic at play is that entities want to control the *assets*, and I don't use the word asset to sound impersonal, but that's exactly what schools, agents, and coaches consider a young athlete who has matriculated into the process. What happens within the dynamics of this industry is that large corporations want to control the assets. It all comes down to a power dynamic.

What we'll see at the grassroots level is that the mega shoe brands are trying to aggregate as many assets as possible. They sponsor "exposure camps" to bring groups of athletically-talented individuals together, and then through their network of partners, coaches, colleges, and agents, they allow their internal network to have a shot at meeting and seeing the players in the early stage of the athletes' talent and capability. It's a perfect storm that consists of an old boys' club that deals exclusively with people inside their brand. Anyone they deem disruptive, they try to seed out very instantly. And let me be clear, I am not bashing the mega-brands, rather I'm merely describing the typical business model in the industry.

Throughout the process, the big brand representatives are typically doing things that are against regulations, but because they try to keep it in their in-house network, they are allowed to get away with it—the old adage "Don't bite the hand that feeds you" is at play. Everyone kind of just goes with the grain instead of against it. Young athletes are put on the conveyor belt and regarded as an asset to these corporations because the corporations want to create opportunity to grow profits. Athletes and parents, and teams and owners, please realize that at the end of the day, the reason the game is played, and the money is generated, is solely because of the athlete. No one goes to their team's games to watch the owner sit in the stands. You go watch them because the stars are performing on the court in a way that only a small percentage of human beings throughout history could accomplish at that level.

Athletes become empowered when they realize that the dynamic is essentially put in place to see how what they do benefits everyone else. An empowered athlete realizes what his service does to support and help the economy thrive. When you play at a high level, you accomplish something that only a select few can do. And don't think for a moment that the powers that be are giving you some magic pill to create an opportunity for yourself, when really you're creating your own opportunity by combining your talent, gifts, drive, and determination.

The current dynamic is a power struggle where brands and teams, leagues, coaches, and agents basically have the mindset that they are the saviors to athletes, instead of presenting themselves as they truly are; a springboard for athletes to showcase their abilities. An empowered athlete realizes his power, and he doesn't allow others to wield unjust power over him. The athlete possesses the power to make his situation a win-win-win opportunity. A win for the athlete, a win for the industry personnel, and a win for the supporting cast, the fans, and the consumers. When people as a whole recognize the win-win dynamic, the industry won't only benefit all of the stakeholders, I believe it will benefit the community at large. Because that's how business should operate. It should be done from a holistic approach, to make whatever we're doing benefit the majority of people, instead of thinking, "How do I do something to benefit myself?", which is currently the dynamic in this industry which says, "What have you done for me lately?"

The current process helps the rich get richer and I don't mean to say that in any type of fuzzy foo-foo way, but the current process makes it where if you're not a major shoe brand or sports apparel entity you're just not important or worthy enough to compete. When you think of the Yankees, you think of the big-name brands. We're so brand dominated and brand-loyal that we allow brands to run the world. It's not even the owners that are running the show; it's the brands controlling the lion's share and that's why everyone has their hand out to get their check from these big brands. The current process continues because everyone keeps doing the same thing which goes along with the well-used idiom, the definition of insanity is when you do the same thing over and over and expect different results. *Assets* at a young age get put on the conveyor belt. Then they're placed on the right travel ball team, whose travel ball team happens to have a major shoe brand logo on their sneakers. The *asset* is sent off to a university who also has that same mega shoe brand logo, and who happens to find the agent who's going to try to make sure he does what is in the best interest for that brand to get himself paid. Finally, the *asset* happens to go into a league that has that same logo.

It's a deeply entrenched process that nobody really wants to change because all the major players, except athletes, have a stake in the monetary gain. Everyone bends to the will of the brand, and only accepts the check they can receive from the brand, instead of holistically solving problems and thinking about what is best for each individual.

ଔ ଓ

The agent/athlete business process is presently moving from sports agent to a business manager who handles all the aspects of the athlete rather than just the role of, "Here, let me find you a team." Rather, it will be, "I'm going to help guide you through sports AND life. God willing, you'll play your sport for 20 years, and if you have a business manager, he should be someone who helps set you up every step of the way, someone who helps you become a legacy for your family, not merely in the financial freedom arena but in achievement and accomplishments.

A crucial pivot is coming, and in modern terms, let's call it a consultant role. For us to get to where it needs to be, we need to take the right steps and follow precise practices of empowering athletes to realize the power of their platform. We need to help them maximize their power, and then apply that personal power to empower others. That's what this book is about—education and empowerment—and it's the underlying motivation for all I do.

I want to educate in the sense of helping you, the athlete, understand what's at play in the world that you want to perform in, and how that world works. I've talked to so many parents and athletes, and it astounds me how ill-informed they are on the process they're about to navigate. They're in desperate need of education to deeply understand what they're getting themselves into. The empowerment piece is knowing how to take what you just learned and then asking yourself, "Exactly how do I maximize the opportunity I've been given to the fullest?"

There are no guarantees in life, so what are you going to do to empower yourself no matter if the process makes you the next star or the next Joe Schmo no one ever hears about?

The uncertainty leads to how important it is to gain the education, which in turn leads to empowerment, which leads to freedom. Because freedom is truly a mindset. A free individual is one who recognizes that freedom is within their own mind, and can take that freedom and apply it to the world in which they live. Don't you see? If we all can be educated, empowered, and recognize our freedom, we will appreciate the value of each individual we interact with, be it the CEO, the janitor, your wife, your kids, your colleagues, and so on. Every person you meet has value, and every person you meet is significant. I'm not saying we'll live in some utopia...the world is the world, and there is always going to be suffering and sacrifice.

The money and the fame don't really matter in the overall picture. My opinion of how money works is that if you're good at something, you work hard enough at it, and you possess some financial intelligence, the money is going to come. As far as fame goes, you can't really control that either.

We've covered a lot of ground in this chapter about the current process and how it operates. I hope it has opened your eyes as to how much is at stake for the athlete. In the next chapter, Goal Three, we'll dig further into each stakeholder's role within the process and learn how each stakeholder can effectively navigate the process to glean maximum benefits.

The Q & A session for Goal Two is with Curtis Madden, former college athlete, and whose son currently plays for Seattle Seahawks. Curtis knows the system intricately!

Q & A Session

Curtis Madden
Former College Athlete
Offensive Coordinator, Dana Hill High School
Father of NFL Player

Q: Tell us a little about your football background.

A: I've been in and around football for about forty-one years. As far as my playing experience, I played at Dennison High School in Texas where we won a state championship my sophomore year, my junior year I was an All-State running back, and my senior year I earned a scholarship to Kansas State and played for Bill Snyder. I have been around some really great football players, and excellent coaches. I could run the list of famous coaches I've been around, anywhere from Edward Orgeron, Brent Venables at Clemson who was a teammate, Bob Stoops who coached at Oklahoma, Lane Kiffin, Pete Carroll, the list goes on and on. And then I've been a coach here in Southern California for the last twenty years.

Q: When did you first notice that your son possessed football talent?

A: I identified it early in his life. Tre was twelve or fourteen months old and we were in the front yard. He had a little toy football and I was trying to teach him how to throw it, and I tossed it to him and he actually caught it. I said, "Now throw it back to daddy," and he says in his toddler voice, "How you do it daddy?" I showed him how to hold the little football and I said, "Now throw it as hard as you can!" I stood about ten feet away from him and he threw the ball fourteen feet over my head, so that's when I thought, *Oh my God I have an athlete on my hands*. Every holiday, every birthday, he got some sort of ball. Baseball, Soccer ball, Football, Basketball, Volleyball; you name it. I bought him golf clubs, a tennis racket—I was always trying to make sure he had some athletic activity in which to get involved. If it wasn't an organized sport, it was a sport-related activity I would do with him. He started playing football pretty early, probably at six years old when we lived in Texas. He was always the fastest kid on the field and actually even before that, I made it a point to stretch him, even as a baby—I'd lay him on his back, take his legs and put them over his head to keep his hamstrings pliable. Family and friends would ask, "*What* are you doing? You're killing your kid!" I retorted, "No I'm not, just watch when he gets older, he'll be the fastest thing moving," and he was.

Having been a D-1 football player myself, and knowing what sort of injuries players sustained, I caught myself getting ahead of the curve. My ex-wife was a very good athlete. She was a track star and basketball player, and I was a track star and football player. My ex-wife's dad is Lawrence McCutcheon, who was an outstanding running back for the Rams in the seventies. On top of that, her brother played for USC and then for the Cleveland Browns. So I knew my son would be blessed with athletic ability, but I also knew it was my responsibility to make sure it wasn't wasted.

Q: Did you notice a stark difference in the system when your son started playing all the youth leagues as opposed to when you were coming up?

A: Yes, I did. Back when I was a kid, parents would come and support, but you had to earn what you got and if you weren't, that means you needed to work harder. When my son started coming through the system, there was more of a sense of entitlement, where parents wanted kids to get participation trophies and a sense of fair play. There was a "rule" called "must-play" where every kid had to play—each kid on the team had to play ten plays to be counted as a legal game. I think it's eroded the game because now there are those who want to give you trophies just to be a part of something. I don't think that's right. I don't think it teaches the right lesson. Sports is about competing and sacrifice. It sets the kid up for failure later. I think the best example of delayed gratification is where you have to set a goal, and you have to work hard to be successful. Not everybody's going to be a champion. Not everybody deserves a trophy. But the lessons that you learn from being an athlete will help you be competitive in life. It helps shape the kind of man or woman you're supposed to be.

Q: How important do you think it is for parents to educate themselves and their student-athlete in the process of succeeding in sports?

A: The most critical aspect of helping an athlete be successful is for his parents to understand first and foremost all the numbers. Let's use football as an example: there are roughly four or five million high school football players in the country. From that four or five million, maybe two or three percent of those players go on to college. Less than a tenth of a percent go on to the pros, so you've got these four to five million kids playing for roughly 1,700 pro positions from the thirty-two pro teams with fifty-three-man rosters for each team. It's simple math. Everybody is not going to play in the NFL! And that's ok. Not everybody deserves to.

Parents have to understand the process as does their kid: if you work hard, your athletic ability can earn you the right to play at the next level. In youth sports, the next level is high school. In high school the next level is college. In college, the reality of it is, that's as far as you're really going to go because it takes a lot of different factors to get you into the pros, and it's not always athletic ability. Knowing the process, parents need to be taught to think like, "How can I get my child into college?" Not everybody is going to go to USC, not everyone's going to Michigan. There are hundreds of colleges and universities in the United States. Not everybody is going to one. There are quality D-2 and D-3 schools out there. Parents need to be able to reassess and set realistic expectations for what their child can accomplish. There is no shame in going to a D-2 or D-3 school.

As a former player and current coach, I can tell you, parents don't really understand. Unless they've played Division One football, they have no idea what's involved. The following is a typical day for a student-athlete: you wake up at five o'clock a.m. to go lift weights at 5:30 a.m., you lift from 5:30 a.m. to 7:15 a.m., you rush back to the dorms, you eat your breakfast, shower, go to class from about 8:30 a.m. to 11:30 a.m., then you go to lunch. After lunch you go to the athletic complex for treatment and then if you didn't lift early in the morning you lift after lunch. Then you have meetings, then you have practice from 4:30 p.m. to 7:00 p.m., then after that you have to get to the training table, then you eat, then you have to go study. That's a full day. It's 10:00 p.m. by the time you're back in the dorms. You have to get some sleep at some point because you've got to start over the next day…and the next…and the next. Repeat that for four years. Everybody can't do that. If your family doesn't have a lot of money you're stuck in the dorms. If you don't have a car, if you don't qualify for a field grant, you can't go to the movies, you can't engage in the normal college experience.

Q: **What is the best way to educate parents so they know what to expect for their student-athlete, how much should they be involved in the process, and how much should the student-athlete be involved?**

A: Of course there is this *G.P.S. Guide* which educates everyone surrounding the athlete, including the athlete himself. There is additional material out there from guys like me who have played at the collegiate level. Those who have played know what to expect. But first things first, parents need to learn how to get their student-athlete into college. A lot of parents think that if their kid gets All-District or All-State, he's automatically going to go to college. No! The first thing recruiters are going to ask about is your core competency GPA. Then they're going to ask, "Have you taken the SAT or ACT?" If you don't have a 2.5 in your core competencies and you haven't taken the SAT or ACT, you're not going to college, especially not D-1. It's not going to happen. It's a process before the process.

The freshman year in high school is the most critical year. Most juvenile males are not mature enough to handle what's required that freshman year. I've seen this hundreds of times where young men will do their homework and not turn it in. It's the craziest thing, but that move in and of itself is what's going to hamper them later on from being able to get into college. Oftentimes parents are so busy chasing "the cheese" that they're not paying attention to what their sons are doing, and the Friday Night Lights glamor has them so enamored, "Oh, look what my Johnny is doing, oh he's going to go play for USC," and they lose focus.

A lot of these young men come from the inner city, and they play football for survival, a way to escape. Down here in South Orange County, California, they play for a hobby.

Q: Is it harder to get the education about the system to the inner-city parents than it is to the big city, urban areas?

A: I think so. They see the pros on Sunday, all the guys with the bling-bling, they get excited because they see the opportunity of being able to play at the NFL level, and how it's going to benefit them.

And don't even get me started on the NCAA. I figure during the course of my career, if I look at radio, television, merchandise, games, concessions, and myself as a member of that team, I probably earned the university about seven to nine million dollars…just me. Multiply that by hundreds of players. Do the math. What "pay" did I get? I got room and board, and I got my scholarship for those five years. My benefit came out to a little under $175,000. The payoff for them was basically thirty times what they invested. So at the end of the day, shouldn't I be entitled to some sort of compensation to help me get started after college?

Q: Describe a frustration or challenge you've experienced as a parent of an athlete.

A: The NCAA slapped sanctions on USC for something that happened when my son was in the sixth grade. The NCAA took thirty scholarships away from them and effectively ruined their chance of competing for a national championship because of something that happened when Tre was in the sixth grade. And I thought that was just crazy. So when the NCAA did that, they allowed the Alabamas and the Oregons and all the other colleges to step up to the stage. I would have to say that as a parent of a college athlete that was by far my biggest frustration. The wonderful thing about all that is that the young men who attended USC after the sanctions, the ones who played with my son, a majority of them made it to the NFL, and I think that was God's way of fixing things.

Q: How did you train Tre to keep the mental focus and fortitude during training, practices, games and life in general?

A: I was hard on him. I was extremely hard on him. We always watched football together and he said to me one day, "Dad, I want to play in the NFL." I replied, "Are you sure that's what you want to do?" He said, "Yeah." So we sat down, I cut the television off, I looked at him eye to eye, and I said, "I need you to promise me that you'll do everything I ask you to do, and at times you're going to hate me, but if you promise, I'll do everything in my power to get you there. I can't guarantee you that you'll stay once you're there but I'll do everything

I can to give you the opportunity." He simply said, "Okay, I promise." It was rough. When I should have been more loving as a father, I was mean. I was physically demanding. I put him in every situation to see how he would respond.

I was a coach on a team that he played on and everyone knew he was the most talented kid in Orange County at the time. The other two guys who played running back ahead of him were threatening to transfer to another team. I told these young men, "No, you stay where you're at, this team was already intact and my son has got to earn his way to that position." I ended up developing a three-person rotation and it made the backfield so competitive that the parents embraced my rotation. Each of the running backs got three plays. If they didn't score a touchdown in those three plays, the next guy was sent in. And if they scored a touchdown, the next two plays they could score again. What I taught my son was, "Just because I'm who I am doesn't entitle you to a position. You have to outwork the other guys to get it." And he did.

Q: Has your son come back and thanked you for being tough on him? After all, he's in the pros now.

A: When he played last year, which was his first year in the NFL, he was on injured reserve. His first preseason game was against the Chargers and after the game everyone rushed down to see him and I just kind of took my time while all the fans hugged him and congratulated him. Someone finally said to me, "Curtis, Tre is over here." I thought, *Yeah, yeah, yeah, whatever, okay.* So I get over to where he was, he sees me, and he gives me a big bear hug and we both started to cry, and he said, "Dad, WE made it!" And that was it. That was the thank you. I was just fine with that.

Q: Describe a specific situation where you had to provide an extra dose of encouragement to your son, maybe during a tough loss or disappointment.

A: Training camp is the worst time in a football player's life and Tre was away from his family and he was going to practice every day, all day, getting beat up, getting mentally assaulted. There are times when you, as a player, ask yourself, "Why the hell am I here? What am I doing this for?" And so I would send him little gems of encouragement; daily wisdom that I would find on Twitter, or certain inspirational sites that have uplifting quotes, or I would, and still do, send him words like, "You know son, I'm so proud of you, you've accomplished more with what you've been given than anyone thought possible. They gave up on you when you got hurt at USC, and look at you now. Go out there and be the baddest guy on the field." His mom would send him Bible verses and encouraging notes. Once he made the Seahawks roster, he said, "Dad, those notes helped a lot more than you realize. Some days I wanted to just give up but your notes and mom's notes helped me through." I knew that as his dad because I've been his dad his whole life and I know my child, and I know when I have to be hard on him and I know when I have to love him up.

My own dad was like that with me. He was always there for me. Now he wasn't the most loving individual and he didn't always tell me he was proud of me, but one day when I was grown I asked him before he died, "Why didn't you ever tell me you were proud of me? Because that's all I ever wanted to hear." He said, "I know, but I also knew if I told you that you would stop trying." "No," I told him.

"Daddy that's BS, because you didn't raise me that way. I just needed to hear it sometimes and know that you really saw me and that you were proud of me as your son." Because that's all little boys want. That's all they want to hear. Little boys always want the acceptance of their father. The approval of their father is paramount. I knew that when it came to both of my kids and so I try to make sure I give them what they need.

Q: So what advice would you give to other parents of promising young athletes looking to advance in their sport?

A: Make sure their grades are on point. Don't allow them to settle for C's or D's. They know what it's like to push themselves and compete on the football field or baseball field or basketball court, so they need to compete in the classroom, and realize they're competing against themselves—they're competing against laziness and lethargy, against success and failure. I tell the student-athletes I coach, "If you don't attack those grades with the same vigor that you attack the weight room or your opponent on the field, you're going to lose."

Q: What's your best tip on how to develop leadership skills because every player needs that in some capacity?

A: Observe someone great, observe a leader who you respect and want to emulate their behavior. Imitation is the best form of flattery so study the Pete Carrolls, the Nick Sabans, the Ed Orgerons, and the Bob Ladouceurs. Watch how they lead their teams, or study the great players like Payton Manning, Troy Aikman, and Tom Brady. And it's not always the guy who yells and screams, you know, the rah, rah, rah guy. Sometimes it's the guy who just buckles up his helmet and leads by example.

When a big play needs to be made, you be the guy to do it. That's a leader.

Q: How does it feel to be a parent of a pro athlete? Your son plays for the Seahawks. How is it as a parent knowing that you've walked with him through the whole journey?

A: I thought it was going to be like this big evolution, this big life-changing, *oh my God my son plays in the NFL* experience. But then I looked at that statement, my son plays in the NFL. My son is still my son. Playing in the NFL is not who he is, it's what he does. If he stopped playing tomorrow, I have 20,000 photos of him and a million memories of him doing incredible things that no one else has claim to. And no one can ever take that from me. If I die tonight, I die a happy man because my son has achieved something that we said we wanted to do.

Intersection of Education and Empowerment

Direction Questions:

Who is on your support team? Name each person and list their role.

If you want to be the next LeBron James, what are you doing daily to improve your skills? Are you dunking 500 times? How are you perfecting your jump shot? Are you practicing your footwork and placement on the court?

Empowerment Exercise:

Take a moment today and thank each person for the time and effort they put in to help you achieve your sports goals. Gratitude is a learned skill and will help you appreciate yourself more, and those in your life.

GOAL THREE

How to Accelerate Toward Maximum Benefits

"The spirit is the true self. The spirit, the will to win, and the will to excel are the things that endure."

~ Cicero

This chapter is personal. Personal to you, that is. You'll undoubtedly find yourself in one of the stakeholder groups that I'll be discussing throughout this chapter. I'll educate each group of stakeholders on how to successfully navigate the process, which will result in empowerment, which is reaping the benefits from learning how to leverage your newly found knowledge.

Before we jump in, though, you'll need to know how I define stakeholders. A stakeholder is anyone associated with the sports world; players, parents, schools and universities, pro sports leagues and teams, sports business professionals, and finally, fans and the community. I'm going to speak to each group directly as if we were sitting across from each other at a dining table in your home, making eye contact, and interacting back and forth.

Let's get into it.

Athletes

The ultimate benefit through learning to navigate is living the life YOU want to live. By understanding where you want to go, and what it takes to get there, that, in my opinion, is freedom. Athletes, you must realize you're in a unique position based on your skill set, to escape the nine to five humdrum, to leave the cubicle lifestyle that many of your peers will naturally gravitate toward. And that's not to say you're better or worse than your peers but using your platform is achieved through realizing where you are today and where you would like to go, and working backwards from there. But as we've talked about, make sure that on day one you know exactly where you stand and where you want to go.

Many business books urge us to find our *why*, and the sports world is no different. Firmly plant your philosophies and values, for they will carry you on your journey. It's important not to put this off until tomorrow. Coaches don't put practices off until tomorrow. You practice today and every day. The same applies to your sports mentality. If you're not clear on what your values and philosophies are, then as I've said, consult with your parents, or a trusted teacher, coach, or mentor.

Parents

Parents can learn how to glean the maximum benefits by being the best support system they can for their student-athlete. Parents, check yourselves at the door and realize that this journey is for your young athlete; this isn't for you to live vicariously through your child. At the end of the day, you're still going to be mom and dad. If you have a little experience that equips you to help with some of the skills training, or you become an agent, that's great, but that scenario is going to be few and far between because most parents don't have the background or skill set to do that. You also benefit by learning how to best support your child through having very frank, open and transparent communication with your child, going back to what your child needs to do as the athlete.

Parents can work hand in hand with their student-athlete to figure out where he is currently, what he wants to accomplish, and what their child's philosophies are that are going to carry them through. By you being in lock step with your young athlete, that's how you'll glean the most benefit, because now you're on the ride with them, and not trying to control or distract them with your own views and opinions. Through discussions and interacting often you realize you're there to support your young athlete.

I'm often asked where parents can go to find trustworthy sources so they can gain the information that they need. Obviously many will go to the top recruiting companies, but keep in mind, not all recruiting companies are created equal. Many of them just want your money—they drastically over promise and under deliver. The important thing to remember is that you have options for input and feedback.

First, you can go directly to the coach. Coaches typically know what's happening in the recruiting world; they know who's who and can aid in steering you away from disreputable and seedy recruiting companies. Another option is that you can visit your youth's school office and talk to a guidance counselor, or other school official. It might also be helpful to visit the NCAA's website and take a look at their resources and regulations.

Go to the specific sports league player unions and, again, look at their rules and regulations, and how they operate. Start on a local level, move upward to regional, and then to the national level. And, don't forget about turning to your student-athlete's peers and their parents who have gone through or are going through the process. The goal in talking to other student-athletes and their parents isn't to compare your child to theirs but to foster a parental support process.

The ultimate goal for researching and talking to each of these entities is to learn as much as you can about their assessment of your child, what resources each entity can provide, and what insights they might have to offer.

Parents, a great deal of the time, find themselves competing more than the players. The players realize *we're in this brotherhood together* but the parents think, *Oh, MY kid has got to be better than YOUR kid, and YOUR kid gets a chance and MY kid doesn't*. What you should realize as a parent is the importance of being a support process within a support process—the ultimate recipe for success is when parents create a win-win supportive dynamic with other parents.

There is also some value in seeking clinical support, a therapist, or maybe even a sports psychologist; someone who can explain to you as a parent what to expect when your child plays sports. Most often the focus of the household is keeping the young athlete in tip top shape but parents also need to put in the work in a personal mindfulness journey. Sharpening yourself individually will then collectively lead to successful interactions with other young athletes, parents, and coaches.

Schools and Colleges

Schools and colleges can glean maximum benefits by relinquishing some control. The big epidemic that's sweeping many colleges throughout the country is that players commit to a school, and then before the school knows it, that same student withdraws their commitment. The school and the students experience a vicious cycle of attendance and withdrawal…attendance and transfer.

At the end of the day, the school must realize their ultimate goal; attract and enroll the most talented young athletes to their school and get them to stay as long as possible. Schools need to put packages in place where they support the athlete and tailor the packages on a case-by-case approach instead of having stringent regulations where they try to lump all the athletes in the same category, when that's simply not the case.

I'm not saying create more work, but enlist flexible rules that demonstrate that the student-athletes coming into the school are individuals, and young individuals at that. When schools and colleges put student-athletes in rigid, controlled boxes, all the school does is create unnecessary friction and the results the school is seeking get lost amongst the rigidity. If schools recognize their role and the power they have, and learn to let go of some of that power instead of being so stringent, they will receive maximum benefits because a more fluid process will yield the end result they want. Schools today often find themselves in a reactive mode when what they really need is to be proactive.

Let's not forget how the NCAA plays into the college picture. We all know they're classified as a non-profit but in all truth, they're in business to make a profit and their business thrives off getting talent, retaining talent, and hopefully getting that talent results. We must get past the illusion that they are trying to provide a service by helping athletes obtain degrees and instead realize that they are in the business of creating partnerships. By partnering with young athletes, by partnering with different schools, coaches and industry professionals, those partnerships can bear the most fruit if everyone has an even interest, an even say in how the process runs.

In my opinion, the NCAA, along with the schools and colleges, want too much control, and they want to use documents to drive the process instead of being more relationally-based. In a sense the NCAA becomes inequitable because they want to make certain people conform to certain views, rules and regulations that, again, may be applicable in one region, but not in another. The NCAA generated a billion dollars last year. They should have practices in place that cater more toward providing service as opposed to controlling the process.

Pro Sports Leagues and Teams

Pro sports teams and leagues can glean maximum benefits while learning how to navigate the process by realizing they are the promised land for student-athletes. Most of these talented individuals will be able to play at the travel ball high school level, and the slight few will get to the college level, and even a smaller portion will get to the pro level. If the pro sports teams and leagues take an interest earlier on, they can discern those who are not going to become athletes and move them toward becoming their ticket sales director, security admin, or the next general manager. Establish a partnership mentality of *we don't just care about how hard you throw a ball, or how far you can shoot a ball through a hoop; we want to make sure we're finding leaders and creating leaders.*

Honestly, for sports teams and leagues it works the opposite of what I'm telling the schools and NCAA to do. While schools and the NCAA need to let go of some control, the leagues and teams need to bring in a little more control because they are the ones that can have the most influence, because at the end of the day, they are the final piece of the puzzle, and the final piece of the puzzle says this is how I want my interns to look, my general managers to look, my athletes to look.

Sports Business Professionals

Sports business professionals can glean the maximum benefits by doing exactly the opposite of anyone else. Today's sports business professional is all about innovation. By being innovative, we create opportunities and will always be looking at how we can push the limit. What is coming next? Not focusing solely on what happened five years ago, or what's happening today, but thinking about how to glean what we project to be in the future and working toward the future process. Most industry professionals look at the past and the current process and try to work within that process instead of creating the next process. Innovation is coming to this world no matter if we're ready or not, and it comes faster and faster as each generation progresses. The more we're open to innovation, and use it to benefit all stakeholders, that's how industry professionals will glean the most value, because we will create that value.

Just to be clear, innovation encompasses scouts, coaches, agents, financial advisors, trainers, and sports psychologists. With technology changes, with physical changes in athletes, with changes in the country and global demographics, innovation is applicable to all, especially sports agents because the industry is getting to the point where athletes want to know what they're paying for. We're moving toward a lot more transparency in finances and athletes aren't going to be as comfortable just handing over X percent without grilling you about what you're doing to earn that amount. So agents can focus on leading with value and recognizing they've earned each athlete client, and not the fact that they've been able to recruit or because of their track record.

The idiom of "flipping the script" is applicable here—agents are not giving X, they are *earning* X. For other sports professionals I'm not saying you need to be a business owner, but you need to be entrepreneurial. If you work for someone, your employer doesn't want to have to tell you what to do all the time. Employers want someone who's going to bring them the next idea and by being entrepreneurial, innovative, a creative thinker, a problem solver, you'll always either be gainfully employed, or you'll create your own business opportunity.

The same principles that apply to sports agents apply to coaches. Learning from the great thinkers in your industry and employing the tactics is how you grow as a coach. It's what will make you a standout coach, a coach your athletes and their parents remember, an influential coach.

Community and Fans

I spoke about players and how they're the most powerful, but here I must mention that they're only the most powerful because of the ultimate powers that be, and those powers that be are consumers. At the end of the day, every business exists to generate money. That money comes from the consumer. When actively engaged consumers understand why and where they spend their dollars, they will influence the world on a large scale.

As a consumer, you spend money in places where you buy into what a particular business is doing and how they're doing it, so in sports it's not simply how hard someone throws a ball, how talented they are, or how fast they run; we ask ourselves how they meet our mission and personal vision.

I want to identify as a fan. A fan at any age can be a fanatic, and age is not a factor on the fan-o-meter; the fan age range spans from Baby Boomers, gen-Xers, Xennials, Gen-Y (Millennials), Gen-Z, and the future Gen Alpha. We do know that fans expect and even demand a more engaging, immersive experience than ever before. So if you're going to act fanatical about something, make sure it's something that you believe in, not just arbitrarily thinking, *wow, this team has the coolest uniforms so therefore I'm going to spend money on that team, on that franchise.*

If fans and the community realize there is a much deeper connection to the game of sports, and how you spend your dollars can exert influence not just in your local community but the global community, if the community and fans realize what is important to them, they can make the industry bend to their will.

Now that's some serious power! And power is meant to be used to create an end result.

☙ ❧

Okay, so we've discussed how each stakeholder can glean maximum benefits from the current process. Now let's peer into the window of not allowing others to take advantage of you within the process.

I'm going to sound like a broken record, but a lot of it goes back to you understanding what you're doing and why you're doing it. You must embrace, I mean *really* own a resilient understanding of your philosophy, your values, and why you're involved in an enterprise in the first place. If you understand your why, your purpose in life, what you want to obtain in this life, and what you want to accomplish in this life, that's the first piece.

Then after the why, it's the what. How do I bring that passion, that purpose to life? After you've established the why and the what, you must look to where you would like to go on this journey and work backwards. The most important thing stakeholders must hold close is to know why they are doing what they are doing, and what they aspire to achieve through their actions.

It's essential that stakeholders gain the knowledge to make sure others' plans align with their own. This piece comes down to research…you have to research a company, a school, an advisor, an agent, a coach to try to glean a third-party perspective on what their brand looks and feels like. Research involves direct contact, communication, and asking honest, pointed questions to determine if synergy exists.

Keep in mind that how you approach a service provider depends on how you seek them out, or if they seek you out. The process could be interchangeable. Transparently tell what your morals are; your values, your pillars, your philosophies. You can't fake your way through this research part.

You know in your heart and mind if you sense a connection to someone, so don't allow yourself to be bamboozled by a sharp image or a track record that appears that the agent or coach helped another athlete or individual succeed because it doesn't guarantee that their image or track record will help you succeed. Depend on your discernment to ask yourself, *is this guy giving me a song and dance, or is he really legit*? Ultimately, people at their core are who they are, and who they are is more important than what they've done. Got it? Good. Let's move on.

I would also add that patience is a big part of the equation. I know the temptation is to succumb to laziness because you just want the process to be over. I can't overstate this enough—don't make decisions based on what you *don't* want to do, make decisions based on what you *do* want to do. In time, individuals show you their true colors. So if you see a nice polished package on day one, that's because that's what they want you to see. Let's see what day two brings, day three, day four. Exercise patience and make sure you're making the right decision…for YOU. Don't over analyze it, but don't rush the process.

"When someone shows you their character, believe them the first time." That adage applies to all agents who are coming at athletes. After all, as an agent, you know you're ethical. You know you're a good guy because your track record has shown your moral and ethical character. But then here comes Mr. Agent Man who *appears* to possess the same moral character… at first. Observe his behavior the second day, at six weeks, at three months and eventually their true colors will appear. The cream will rise to the top, but the clunky ones weighted with false promises and broken commitments, which there are plenty of, will reveal themselves soon enough, and sink to the bottom of the character pool.

Most people who are selling you something want you to hurry up and buy. How many times have you heard this phrase at a car dealership, "How can I earn your business?" I love taking the complete opposite perspective on almost anything. My phrase is "How do I lose your business?" Let me walk this walk with you long enough and I'm comfortable and confident enough in my process that I'll take some losses, I'll take some wins, but at the end of the day, I'm going to lead with value. I don't want to merely convince you, sell you, and win your business, because that's just sales, that's just fluff. That's not authenticity. Authenticity is being there with an athlete each step of the way, and if at any point that athlete wants to get off the off-ramp, that's fine.

As an agent, I want you to sit, reflect, discern, and commit, which is a much different approach because I'm not selling me. I'm empowering athletes through educating them, and trying to establish a partnership so they can navigate their athletic career on a top-shelf level. And this is why patience is so important! Partnerships, whether business, sports, marriage, or otherwise, are not formed overnight.

Compass Required — Navigating the Process

Again, I can't stress it enough—navigating through the athletic process starts by knowing who you are. And by knowing who you are, you're able to determine your philosophies, your values, and the moral pillars you live by. Knowing who you are will guide you on what you want to do, with whom, and how you want to carry out your plan. The best resource you can tap into to empower yourself is your own internal compass!

Once you have taken the time to truly know and understand your core, to embrace the characteristics that make you a distinctive individual, you'll start leading by example, thus become more acutely aware of industry leaders who seek to have a vested interest in your athletic journey.

We've established in this chapter that it takes serious honest reflection to start navigating around the process. Educating yourself on the process, on current events within your sport, on regulations, and then taking time to reflect on everything, you'll understand how to best sharpen yourself. Often, when you're well into the process of examining yourself, who you started out thinking you are and who you truly are aren't aligned. The goal is to align your thoughts and your actions so they work in unison because *that's* your authentic self. Learn as much as you can, apply your knowledge, and as a result, you'll live an authentic life; an example for others to follow.

It's been said you can't know where you're going without knowing where you've been. With that in mind, in order to recognize how an empowered process can revolutionize and revitalize the process, we must first highlight the flaws and negative results, intended or unintended, from the current process. Chapter Four will peel back the curtain to expose just that; the long-standing flaws that have kept the current process on autopilot for so long. My guess is that you'll see what Dorothy saw in the famed movie The Wizard of Oz when her little dog Toto yanked back the curtain of the great and powerful Oz to see a small, frail, elderly man wildly wielding the control. My hope is that once you peer behind the curtain of the current process's flaws, you'll also see the illusion, and join in to help create a new, empowered process with progressive sustainability.

In our Q & A session for Goal Three we gain an important perspective as Howard Douglas talks about his experience as a financial advisor for athletes within the system. Howard's concise advice will help you navigate in the right direction if you desire to break into the athletic system on the professional side.

Intersection of Education and Empowerment

Direction Question:

What are your personal values, philosophies, and code of ethics as a stakeholder?

Do you have a personal vision statement?

Empowerment Exercise:

Make a list of the qualities that make you distinctive, and state next to each quality how you live out that quality on a consistent basis. If you've been slacking on a particular quality, determine how you will get back on track, and start today to put that quality ingredient back in your life mix.

If you don't have a vision statement, create one using your personal values and core beliefs. It doesn't have to be long, just one or two sentences.

Q & A Session

Howard Douglas
Morgan Stanley, Financial Advisor Associate

Q: Tell a little about yourself and how you help your clients.

A: I was born and raised in Los Angeles, California and I'm a former college athlete. I earned my Bachelor's degree in Business Finance, along with a minor in Economics at West Virginia State University. While at WVSU, I played two years on the Division II Men's Basketball team, and one year on the Men's Tennis team. I'm a proud member of Kappa Alpha Psi. I help athletes, sports professionals, and small business owners make confident financial decisions.

Q: How long have you been a financial advisor for athletes?

A: Specifically for athletes it's been two, going on three years. I've been working in the finance business for just about four years, and I studied finance in college for four years. I like to tell myself eight years total, and gaining strength each day going forward.

Q: Where did you first meet Michael and what were your initial thoughts about his character?

A: I first met Michael through a sports agent back when I was still competing as an athlete. My goal at that time was to play professional basketball in the NBA or overseas. We hit it off immediately, and, as a matter of fact, I helped Michael move into his first apartment in Los Angeles when he first came out here, fresh out of Ohio, and we've been friends as well as business associates ever since. Speaking to his character, Mike is extremely thoughtful, very detailed, hard worker, and his heart is in the right place.

Q: Describe some challenges you've experienced while building your financial advisor business, serving athletes.

A: One of the challenges, and this pertains to the general public too, boils down to lack of education. When there's a high-profile athlete within the family, there are a lot of people soliciting themselves to that athlete and their families, not to say that's a bad thing, if done for the right reasons. A significant task of mine is connecting from a distance to the families and building a relationship so that once those blue-chip athletes do get an opportunity to play professional sports, they have their team together, and they're not behind the financial eight ball. I've had some success creating true unified financial game plans but the ratio is still off because so many more need to put a plan in place *before* they go pro, not *after* they go pro. I know of a handful of professional football players who have played in the NFL for one to three years and don't yet have a financial advisor. That's a recipe for disaster down the road.

It's one of those things where, *you don't know what you don't know*. You don't know the questions to ask, you don't know the skills, resources, or services that an individual or a company provides, it may be the first time the family has engaged with these professionals, and it can be difficult especially with the "noise" from other persons in the situation. Bottom line, I would stress and encourage families to work hard, ask questions, research, and develop a holistic plan that includes finances but other goals as well before the young person gets that once in a lifetime opportunity.

Q: What is the greatest satisfaction for you?

A: The greatest satisfaction is to know that I've made an indelible impact on an athlete and their family, knowing that their financial affairs are in order. An athlete will likely not be thinking, "Hey, if I get injured and I don't get another opportunity, where am I going to be financially? I've banked on a certain salary and if things don't pan out, where does that leave me?" There are a lot of scenarios: the athlete could lose his scholarship opportunity or find himself as a one-and-done in the pros, or if he played X amount of years as a pro, and made X amount of dollars, and then gets injured. If I have helped that athlete execute a specific business plan and investment opportunities, and he is more confident about stepping away from the game, I have done my job. If he wants to go back to college or if he wants to start a business, he can do it responsibly because we planned for it *ahead* of time. It's no fun not having a plan when life takes unexpected turns. You don't want to be that guy who wasted his opportunity. So the greatest satisfaction is making sure that an athlete's financials are in order, and to help athletes and their families make contributions to the things they care about, whether it's philanthropic or family specific.

Q: Do you find that a few parents with student-athletes going into college sometimes have dollar signs in their eyes in their quest for their child to hit the pros and make mega-millions?

A: It's been a mix for me so far. I'll come across parents who may not be financially literate, but they're disciplined, and they want to make sure they have a solid game plan for their kids. I'll come across a few parents who believe their kid is the next best thing and it's my job to educate them on the financial pitfalls of the pros. Then I'll come across some who are business professionals or owners and know how to vet professionals like myself out, or they may choose not to whether that's due to other reasons or procrastination. Everything goes back to education and engagement. I've redirected my strategy and now I focus on a more subtle way of educating, similar to what Michael is doing with this book, because with a book parents can educate themselves, and student-athletes can educate themselves through a self-study effort instead of me making individual phone calls which can most often be very time-consuming.

Q: What has your experience been like working with athletes?

A: Athletes are people. So at the end of the day I believe it begins with trust. And the only way you build trust is through spending time together, building a bond and relationship from a meaningful place, and bringing value on an as-needed basis. For me, it's been an evolutionary process. I didn't understand the business, but through the process of making mistakes, refining my skills, asking the right questions, finding mentors, and just getting after it, I've made a lot of progress. I'm getting closer to my professional goals and making a difference for clients.

Q: What are your short- and long-term business goals as a financial advisor?

A: My short-term business goal includes continuing to grow a sustainable practice of value to my clients. Right now I have close to fifteen total clients and I want to grow that to forty or fifty; predominantly athletes and business owners. I'd also like to bring value to the community and the charitable endeavors I care about. As for my long-term goals, I want to make sure my clients are financially free; a legacy to build on their own.

Q: What advice would you give to business professionals looking to break in to working with athletes?

A: I would say have a strategy, find mentors, and put in the work. Those are the core principles with which I run my life and business life. I think it boils down to having a strong work ethic and showing up. Showing up has so much to do with where you are and where you end up. For me, showing up consistently with the resources, or lack thereof, allowed me to continue climbing, and now things are looking more fruitful compared to when I started. It's one thing to have the best business plan written up on your laptop, but if you don't go out there and meet people and put in the work, then all you're doing is wasting your time and you're wasting other people's time.

Q: How do you keep mental strength through the ups and the downs of your business?

A: There are a lot of ups and downs. I try to decompress at the end of the night by listening to some smooth jazz and lighting some candles. Other than that, I look at my vision board from time to time, and I look myself in the mirror and have honest conversation with myself. Those things give me the affirmation I need to persist.

Q: How do you create your vision board? What does it look like? Is it a PowerPoint? Poster board? Binder?

A: My wife and I bought some frames from Wal-Mart and removed the pictures. We have a whole stack of magazines such as *Black Enterprise* or *Success* or *Essence* and we find pictures that inspire us and demonstrate who we are and where we want to be; we cut those up, paste them on or put them in the frame, and voila, we now have a bunch of nice frames with the things we care about, and the things that motivate us. Pictures of Barack and Michelle, pictures of a husband, wife, and a small baby. Stuff like that. Empowering words. Looking at these photos daily refreshes me and reminds me that I've got to live a good life.

Q: If you had an athlete client sitting in front of you right now, what would you tell him?

A: The first thing I do is educate and empower my clients just as Michael is doing in this book. Number two, I set up their fundamentals and protections, not the big, shiny investment. For example, we determine if they have the right amount of disability insurance. In minor league baseball, they just might hand you that bonus check. What happens if you have Tommy John surgery before they renew for your next contract? You're year to year in baseball until you get through the first three to five years I believe. Does it make sense to get term or whole-life insurance? What type of trust account makes sense for you?

Do you need umbrella insurance to protect you if you're found liable in a lawsuit because you are now a visible target? I wade through the array of people claiming that they have the best interest for him, which they may or may not, and I focus on how to truly connect with my client. Unfortunate events happen all the time—it's not a matter of *if*, it's a matter of *when*. Number three: I set up a strategy for taxation. Not only are you earning a higher amount of money, Uncle Sam is going to be there with his hand out, and you're going to get taxed in every state you play. I work in conjunction with the athlete's tax professional to find strategies to mitigate the tax liability. Everyone has to pay taxes, so it's vital to employ strategic approaches in order to maximize every dollar earned. Number four is budgeting and investments, which I typically group with step three—living well within reason and principle. Making solid investment decisions that make sense for you, not your family or friends, or the television infomercial. Making solid investment decisions also involves *not* giving in to every "great opportunity," [Howard says this sarcastically] or buying a certain stock because you received a notification on your phone app or email says it's taking off. You must have your strategy in place and work that strategy to your best advantage. You may have a family member who has a business idea and asks you for $25,000 and all you've received is a one-million-dollar check from your first time around. Or, you want to buy your parents a house, and you want to buy yourself a house, and you have to move the whole family because not everybody is doing well; that's a lot of responsibility and family pressure. I'm not saying to *not* help your family out, but what I am saying is, you need to know how to plan for your family within reason, and sometimes that may mean saying "no." If I can get through to the athlete or the family and educate them before things get too crazy, we can prevent some of these issues and abuses that happen. Athletes need somebody in their corner who's not afraid to tell them, "No, I don't think that's a good idea." After all, who's going to tell you no when everybody's cheering your name?

Q: What are common mistakes professional athletes make, or myths they believe?

A: Number one is handing off their financial affairs 'blindly' to a family member, friend, or professional. Don't let that happen; you can't be blind. I don't mind having a family member as a key decision-maker on how to budget or plan, not at all, I welcome invested parents. Sometimes abuses happen right in front of you, so that's why I press for "literacy." An athlete or influential family member might experience hesitance, lack of self-confidence, or procrastinate when it comes to their financial matters, and this may or may not be self-inflicted due to how money was treated or not treated in their household. However, this kind of thinking leaves liability for huge mistakes such as not getting started (known as "opportunity cost"). Some of the liabilities include not addressing financial gaps due to not asking the right questions, and lack of vetting a financial professional because you didn't prioritize properly. It's essential to build a relationship with the individual(s) gatekeeping your (family's) wealth and not handing your money over to someone simply because your agent, business manager, or accountant has a relationship, yet you don't know the advisor personally. Remember…it's *your* money. Another gap is having too many "yes" people and no professional sounding board.

Number two is the myth surrounding investing into private-only investments versus public-only investments. The myth is that in private investments you retain more control, which is somewhat true, and that public investments such as stocks and bonds carry an increased risk because they carry an element of uncertainty, therefore you feel uncomfortable, which also could be true. However, the underlying fact, if you are thinking like this, you are fearful and probably lack knowledge, which ties into the *not getting started* response, and not vetting, listening, and getting a suitable team together. The investing myth is inaccurate. If the athlete and his family have the right investment manager/financial advisor, the advisor will understand what the family is looking for, and will purchase investments not on hype or popularity but on true intrinsic value. Value derived from fundamental analysis and process means you are purchasing ownership shares in companies at discounted fair costs versus buying premiums on companies in which you have no idea who they are or what they're doing, but you like the brand or phone application. Liking the brand and app is cool and all, but just because you have an app on your phone and you use it all the time, doesn't make it a good investment. As for the other side of the coin, private investments often lack one of the following: the right corporate or financial structure, the right team spearheading the business, and they often lack liquidity. This doesn't make it a wrong investment, but these risks are often overlooked.

Number three says if it's more expensive, it must be bigger and better, but reality dictates that bigger isn't always better, and neither is more expensive always an indication of a superior quality, whether it is goods or services. The bottom line is value; you do not want to overpay for a good, service, or asset based on familiarity, popularity, or the assumption you could get it for less money. Athletes often get charged higher fees and accounts are churned by not paying attention—this goes back to checks and balances, and value. If the value is justifiable for the higher expense that's okay, but if not, you are paying for someone else's mortgage unjustifiably. On the flip side, from a goods or service standpoint, just because that good or service is offered at a discount doesn't mean it represents equal value to something at standard or premium rates. The name of the game is value, and sound decision-making.

GOAL FOUR

Learn Why the Current Process has Veered Off-Track

"Whenever you find yourself on the side of the majority, it is time to pause and reflect."

~Mark Twain

Don't mistake my exposing the flaws in the current process for pessimism or negativity, for it's the reality of what already exists, and has existed for decades. To improve, we must first take a hard look at the flaws that are stopping athletes from achieving their full potential and successfully navigating through the process to live empowered lives on and off the field and court.

I'm going to refer to these flaws as "side streets" because you know how you can be going along on your route and then you take a wrong turn, get off-track, and end up on a side street that leads to a dead end, or worse yet, blocks you into a neighborhood where you have no business being.

Side Street #1:

I think the main side street of the current process is that it's extremely money-driven. A top-down approach reveals that teams want to spend as little money as possible to get the most valuable asset possible. Educational institutions have limited resources so they consume those resources in almost the same capacity as the teams; they want to gain a lot and pay very little at the grassroots, high school and collegiate levels. The "wooers" as I'll call them pay a lot of money to influence the players and their parents at each level, taking money in ways they shouldn't. This, in turn, creates a negative environment where, as we're seeing in the current sports climate, agents and other powers that be are getting found out and prosecuted for their underhanded deals.

I know full well it's a business, but the general paradigm for teams and personnel directors within those teams must shift from being money-driven, acquiring players simply for the sake of acquiring players, and basically buying people who are, by the way, no longer referred to as people, but products. I've heard first-hand international teams say it straight up: *We have x amount of money to buy a player.*

Listen up: You're not *buying* a player. You're not *buying* a human being. That sounds eerily like the slave trade or human trafficking. You're buying a service. And by purchasing a service, you need to service the person you're getting that service from. Don't just think about it as one million dollars buys me player X. Instead, think of it like, one million dollars gets me a three-point specialist who can also defend, so I should look to that "service provider" to provide services that support him being that three-point specialist who can also defend.

It's flawed thinking to view potential service providers from a purchasing power standpoint instead of viewing them as a resource with which to grow and empower your team, your club, or your organization.

I would be remiss if I didn't mention on this side street the obscene profits the NCAA is making off the backs of student-athletes. In a financial statement for the fiscal year ending Aug. 31, 2017, the NCAA[1] reported $1.045 billion in total revenue—$1.045 BILLION! Talk about money-driven! To top that off, we all know that the NCAA is a 501(c)(3) organization, so it doesn't pay federal income taxes. Must be nice.

I must also bring attention to the blatant hypocrisy of the NCAA and how it deals with one sport over another.

---

[1] http://www.ncaa.org/sites/default/files/2016-17NCAAFin_FinancialStatement_20180129.pdf

In 2016, Texas swimmer Joseph Schooling was paid $753,000 by his native Singapore for winning a gold medal at the Olympics. He got to keep the money because in August 2015 an NCAA policy went into effect that allowed international student-athletes to accept medal bonuses from their countries' equivalents of the United States Olympic Committee (USOC). According to that rule, Schooling was able to accept the gold medal bonus without forfeiting his eligibility.

In 2012, then-amateur swimmer Missy Franklin won five medals, four of which were gold and worth $25,000 in prize money each from the United States Olympic Committee. Franklin wasn't allowed to accept the full financial benefits of her Olympic performance, but she was allowed to keep some of the money. The NCAA allows athletes to accept money earned through the USOC's Operation Gold program, which gives money to athletes based on their performance at high-level competitions such as the Olympics or World Championships.

Per NCAA bylaws: An individual (prospective student-athlete or student-athlete) may accept funds that are administered by the U.S. Olympic Committee pursuant to its Operation Gold program. *(Adopted: 4/26/01)*

What I'm wondering is: Why are Olympic "amateur" swimmers allowed to collect partial or full prize money for excelling in their sport and yet "amateur" football and basketball players are not allowed to receive food money or any other compensation for their performance on the field or court?

According to a cbssports.com article[2], "Ah, but buy lunch for a 14-year-old budding point guard on the AAU circuit and we've got a major problem."

The obvious point to look at here is that swimming is not a profit sport like football or basketball so the NCAA can wink, nod and turn its attention to other pressing items like whether or not an NCAA football player made a call to his mama from his coach's office, a clearly spelled out NCAA rule violation. It's glaringly obvious that overwhelming reforms need to be made, and there is a lot of fat that needs to be cut. Enough said for now…Let's move ahead…

Side Street #2:

Another side street in the current process is that it is extremely superficial. Sports is supposed to be a free market. It's supposed to be open competition. But at the end of the day, especially for athletes who are trying to go on to college and play at a professional level, a lot of it is based on a "rack 'em and stack 'em" mentality. And I'm not saying compiling lists of prospects isn't needed because it is, but it's more about the process of evaluating and determining the prospect's value as it should not be merely based on an opinion, or statistical analysis, or their physical appearance. There needs to be a process that's more thoughtful, more mindful, a more all-encompassing method that evaluates the whole prospect as a human being, and not just a name on a page because each person is uniquely different and the process should reflect responsiveness to each individual's distinctive qualities and needs.

---

[2] Dodd, Dennis, "NCAA's hypocrisy toward revenue-generating sports is more apparent than ever" https://www.cbssports.com/college-basketball/news/ncaas-hypocrisy-toward-revenue-generating-sports-is-more-apparent-than-ever/ (Accessed 8/31/2018).

Side Street #3:

The sports culture runs on X's and O's so our belief is that we need to use X's and O's in running it, instead of navigating and innovating throughout the process as the world changes with us. The ultimate loser in that way of thinking is the young athlete. Those who are employed by the NCAA, the teams, the internal and external business people, they're still more than likely going to have a job. They're still going to have an opportunity if they make a mistake. They're still likely going to grow as a professional. But take that young AAU athlete who makes one or two false missteps; colleges are gone. Forget about pro ball. Forget even the high school level. Their room for error is so, so small as opposed to other industry professionals who can have a couple of misses and still maintain their career. But the young athlete, when they're making these big decisions on how to navigate, are not afforded the same luxury of having missteps.

Side Street #4:

A side street and unintended dead end of the current process is that after players have been playing at the pro level, are at the end of their career, displaying a diminished quality of service, and they aren't bringing in dollars anymore, they're shown the door and discarded like an old sock. It's *Go on your way, Johnny. We don't need you anymore because you're not creating revenue for us.*

Why I say it is an unintended dead end is because at the root I don't think the leagues and schools are evil people who sit around and say, *Ha, ha, ha, we're sucking the value out of all these people*. The truth is that young athletes and families are placed on the sports conveyor belt at a young age, and everyone just depletes them. And once athletes are completely depleted, and their value is taken, they are left to the side, and the next star comes in to take their place. What I think IS intended is when owners, teams, and leagues ensure through setting rules and regulations that the ones who hold the power retain the power, and the service providers who exist to be bought and sold and traded, stay powerless, because those in charge want to control how the process runs, instead of having partnerships with the service providers.

Estimated Probability of Competing in Professional Athletics[3]

Men's Basketball:

NCAA Participants: 18,712

Approximate # Draft Eligible: 4,158

Draft Picks: 60

NCAA Drafted: 50

% NCAA to Pro: 1.2%

---

[3] Sources: High school figures from the 2016-17 High School Athletics Participation Survey conducted by the National Federation of State High School Associations; data from club teams not included. College numbers from the NCAA 2016-17 Sports Sponsorship and Participation Rates Report.

Men's Baseball:

NCAA Participants: 34,980

Approximate # Draft Eligible: 7,773

Draft Picks: 1,215

NCAA Drafted: 735

% NCAA to Pro: 9.5%

Football:

NCAA Participants: 73,063

Approximate # Draft Eligible: 16,236

Draft Picks: 253

NCAA Drafted: 253

% NCAA to Pro: 1.6%

Stats don't lie. Even NCAA president Mark Emmert gave ample time to the issue during his most recent state of the association address, saying that "athletes often have incredibly unrealistic perceptions of their professional prospects."

By displaying the stats and showing you the evidence, I want to show you that there is more opportunity out there in sports business than being a player, agent, coach, or general manager. An NCAA television ad and poster campaign advertises that "there are 400,000 NCAA student-athletes, and almost all of them will go pro in something other than sports.[4]" Our understanding of the odds will help a select few beat the odds and help others refine the odds for success by their own standard.

Say you're one who has beat the odds and now you're an athlete moving full steam ahead on the conveyor belt. You're a cog in the process's wheel. You're one of the fortunate ones (based on the statistics above) who's made it to the pro level and you're being utilized for your talent and being paid well for that talent. Now it's time to use the process to your advantage. Leverage your job title as an athlete! Go talk to the owners of your team. Go talk to the General Manager. You have more power than you think. When you own the title of pro athlete no matter what sport you're in, use the process to advance your education, your influence, your industry connections, and your future.

The sad part is that most athletes don't do this. I'm sure there are a plethora of reasons why; you might not feel like it's your place, you might feel intimidated, you might feel like your words will fall from your mouth like dry and dusty tumbleweeds, or you might even feel scared that the higher ups will shoo you out of their office with a flick of their wrist and wincing scowl. But at the end of the day, you have just as much right to leverage who you know to position yourself for greatness outside the stadium. After all, you have a vested

---

[4] New, Jake, "A Long Shot" https://www.insidehighered.com/news/2015/01/27/college-athletes-greatly-overestimate-their-chances-playing-professionally (Accessed 8/30/2018).

interest in what happens on the field, in the locker room, and beyond the gridiron or court or wherever you compete.

By recognizing your interconnectedness, and the fact that we are *all* powers that be, we *all* have a stake in the process. That's how we truly make the process benefit all stakeholders.

As stakeholders, we embody the entire free market. Pull yourself up by your bootstraps; if you're talented enough, if you're good enough, you'll be granted opportunity. However, the current process is riddled with so many limitations and barriers to the process that, again, only a select few are going to reach the promised land. But we make it even more difficult for that select few to get there and stay there because of all the hoops and loops they must jump through, with the added necessity of adhering to regulations that are arbitrary.

In other industries, be it tech, fashion, pharma, barbering, or veterinary, pretty much anything that exists in business that I can think of, if you're talented, you have opportunities to succeed, and that allow you to get paid for your talent. And, believe me, companies spend big bucks on wooing college students, whether student-athlete or not.

An article in Harvard Business Review[5] succinctly "educates" employers on how to attract the best college talent. Major points of the article include the following:

companies getting their best people to engage with students; going where the students are, which is not necessarily job fairs; making the application process easy and engaging; and prioritizing meaning over swag.

---
[5] Agrawal, Sanjeev, "How Companies Can Attract the Best College Talent" https://hbr.org/2014/03/how-companies-can-attract-the-best-college-talent (Accessed 8/30/2018).

In the sports world, you can be talented, but because of the regulations and rules, you're unable to fully maximize your talent because the NCAA rules you ineligible if an agent, trainer, or coach gives you a free service, gifts, guidance or anything else for that matter. In contrast, in any other industry, people are always available to sharpen you up and make you more marketable for the ultimate end goal.

Taking it a step further, if a non-athletic student is talented and wants to work as an engineer for a better institution, guess what? They can go to college at fifteen years old, and then find employment doing engineering work at sixteen years old.

My point is: non-sport industries don't have arbitrary age restrictions. With that said, I understand in sports there are certain age qualifications and physical maturity criteria, but at the end of the day, as long as a person's body can physically withstand whatever is occurring, I think it should be a case-by-case determination.

I am not saying an eight-year-old should be a linebacker in the NFL, but hypothetically speaking, if there's an eight-year-old who's two hundred and thirty pounds and looks and acts like a grown man, there is a school of thought that says he shouldn't be restricted to play. Now, don't freak out and think I'm advocating that husky eight-year-olds should be playing professional sports. I'm merely painting a picture to portray that if a student-athlete meets all the criteria, they should have the potential to obtain that linebacker or offensive line job.

Here's another way to think about it: A non-athlete individual in college can be courted by a large firm or brand,

and the company flies them in and out, accompanies them on interviews, and brings in representatives on the ground to wine and dine them. Conversely, a student-athlete can be high on a recruiter's list, a team can bring them in for a workout and that student-athlete is not allowed to have other stakeholders come and invest in them and guide them.

The process itself creates an environment of fear for all involved. A player might think *Uh oh, a coach bought me a Coke at a convenience store. That means I could be ruled ineligible*, and they would be absolutely correct. But again, the thing I want to keep bringing up is that decisions should not be made out of fear. Decisions should be made out of creating opportunity for that which we aspire. Not because of what we are afraid of.

Things we are afraid of are still going to occur, so by being proactive, and taking steps to mitigate those fears, or those unsavory ultimate outcomes, we can truly create a better dynamic. The current process puts so much regulation and red tape in place that those unsavory results of disqualification, losing one's scholarship, and ultimately losing out on a pro career are still happening, and it's only creating more losers on the young athlete side.

The rising young star who lands that great job at Google can rise through the ranks and a whole slew of other opportunities open to them, but an athlete has a superficial value of physically providing one service. Once the athlete can no longer provide that service, where do they go?

Perhaps you've heard of the story surrounding Michael Jordan, that once his playing days ended, he went to the Bulls organization and wanted to be a part of how they ran their organization, and was laughed out of the room. Michael Jordan was one of the best players of all time yet he was still seen as, *this is your skill, don't try to do anything else.*

And we see it even now, where a FOX News reporter told LeBron James to "shut up and dribble." Athletes continue to be put in a box that no one else is being put into, and are not allowed to flourish and grow. And when they attempt to grow and expand, they're being snapped back down to their athlete size with "Do what I say."

So when you compare what happens in the sports industry to any other industry, you see the hypocrisy, you see the restriction of the free market, and it's distressing.

It's going to take candid conversation, honesty, and transparency. We must always be conscious of the conveyor belt because it's obviously the young athletes and their support network who are on it, but guess what, the stakeholders are a part of the conveyor belt too because they've supported the athlete along his journey.

The last thing I want to highlight is that no one part of this puzzle controls the whole process yet many want to artificially influence how the process plays out, and those imposters believe they have control. And once we learn to relinquish this false sense of control, and realize how the conveyor belt process can benefit us all, that's when that conveyor belt becomes a network of hands that extends across the table, linked with each other to create opportunities that help us thrive as a species.

Allow me to draw one final bit of attention to the inconsistency and hypocrisy of the "amateur" to the professional sports business process. In America, we believe and embody the principles of freedom in an open, equal, and fair market, but essentially the sports industry is by no means an open, equal, and fair market. There are the Big Three—Rules, Regulations and Red Tape—that restrict how the sports industry runs. I believe the Big Three is resulting in exactly the opposite of what the American pillar of freedom and a free market embody. The process doesn't seem to make any logical sense other than going back to the element of power and those who think they own that power over the process. They brandish their supremacy wand to their ultimate benefit, not realizing that by relinquishing some of their perceived power, and understanding that they never truly owned it in the first place, they can be instrumental in helping create a process that benefits all the stakeholders.

It's vital that a new process be put in place, one that values collaboration and giving a voice to all key stakeholders. Now that would be the most fair and equal method while providing the maximum value for all involved.

Okay, so now you're well aware of the side streets and inconsistencies within the current process, and I hope it has opened your eyes on the reality of what's really behind the curtain of the great and powerful Oz: Feeble, frail, greedy men, each wielding their self-imposed illusion of clout and control.

Intersection of Education and Empowerment

Direction Questions:

What is your plan to gain traction by creating and maximizing your opportunities through the navigation process, wherever you are in that process?

What is the biggest issue you see happening at the point where you are on the conveyor belt?

Empowerment Exercise:

Think of someone who holds power in your stakeholder sphere. Make a phone call and open the lines of communication. Engage the person in candid, honest communication, and it wouldn't hurt to jot down a few notes before the conversation.

Q & A Session

Michael McGinnis, J.D.
Founder of Empowerment Sports Group

Q: Who are you and what company do you represent?

A: My name is Michael McGinnis, and I'm the founder of Empowerment Sports Group and an MLB draft advisor and sports consultant.

Q: What prompted you to become an advisor/agent?

A: The biggest thing I realized and what motivated me was that the individuals who were guiding, advising, and representing athletes were very confident, very knowledgeable, and doing a decent job. But I felt the missing piece was that agents were essentially securing their job security, either intentionally or unintentionally, by keeping their clients very distant and by not properly informing them throughout the business process. Agents were basically safeguarding all their knowledge and power while telling the client to play ball and leave the business to the agent. From that, I found there was a need to educate and inform athletes and their families on what becoming a Division One scholarship athlete entailed. Athletes and their parents didn't know what it took to navigate from grassroots youth sports and Little League, all the way to the pro level, and honestly, these days the game is getting more and more competitive with youth athletes advancing earlier and earlier. So I felt there was an educational piece that was lacking and that the education was what would empower athletes to achieve far greater success during their journey. My revelation caused me to throw my hat in the ring and become a steward for these athletes, making sure they are informed and educated and empowered to make well-informed decisions.

Q: Why did you decide to become an independent agent versus working with a large agency?

A: My original dream was to get picked up by one of the large agencies as I was getting my sports management degree and a law degree but it's a competitive space, and there are not a lot of openings and opportunities; it took me four and a half years just to get an unpaid internship. The industry embodies who you know or what value you can bring to a more prominent firm. After beating my head against the wall for so many years and finally being forceful enough to get an internship and progressing through that role, I worked hand in hand with the agent on scouting, recruitment, and development. I ultimately realized that a smaller operation would allow for better connection and overall more effectiveness as opposed to a large corporate brand. Me not being able to get my foot in the door of a larger agency and finally gaining experience with a few smaller boutique firms, a light bulb went off when I realized I wanted to be a sports advisor and not just an agent. I recognized that through my credibility, my education, and my working life experience, I had all the credentials and was capable of creating an agency myself. That revelation propelled me to form my company as opposed to taking the other path with a large agency that I felt would make me like everyone else. I'm not saying that other agents are wrong, but if they were so amazing and they were doing their jobs so well, the industry would not be full of athletes in financial turmoil and the current dysfunction that has led to the FBI investigation into college basketball. Organically, I got to the place where I'm supposed to be which was taking the road less traveled.

Q: Did you experience any frustrations or challenges in your early days of being an advisor/agent?

A: Absolutely. Some agents have more or better clientele or just better access, yet that access isn't based on the agent's merit. It is based on the alleged star power and/or ability to turn a player into a star that is perceived by athletes and families. The decision to hire an agent wasn't based on who the better person was to represent the client, or because the metrics on a chart demonstrated the agent was more valuable. More often than not it was because that agent had a connection to someone in high places. In the beginning, I was all right with getting beaten out of client applicants because I realized I was losing to agents who were more capable of doing the job than myself…but the funny thing is that my perception was that those agents were winning the clients because they said they had helped another athlete, or that they had a connection to someone who could make things happen for the athlete. The truth is that there was no merit or proof they were good at being an advisor for a client and teaching them the business aspects of the industry. So that was a bit of frustration on the front end—losing through circumstances that were truly outside my control, and to be honest, very arbitrary.

Q: Describe your experience working as an advisor/agent.

A: It's been wonderful! The challenges, the growth, the development I've experienced on a personal level has been invaluable. I feel that personally I've become more compassionate, more empathetic, more able to listen and understand where someone is coming from, where they're trying to go, and help them develop plans to get there, because a lot of the skills I've developed over the years, I now use to empower athletes through the sports process. I've seen such tremendous growth in myself both personally and professionally, and I'm grateful for all the lessons, all the difficulties, and some of the successes because the sports industry is more of an industry of failure. Professionally I feel as if I've gained confidence in realizing that I've lost some, I've won some, but I've learned a lot through the process. I'm now able to focus on being a business advisor and not merely an agent because the industry is ripe for a very dramatic evolution that's in the making. For the last few years, I've been trying to predict and work on the changes on the horizon that will transition agents into more athlete advisors as opposed to the current model where they're viewed as decision-makers. I think the agent industry is going to become more advisory and assistance-driven as opposed to execution regarding exclusively handling the athlete's affairs.

Q: Share a few of the results have you produced for your clients.

A: I've helped clients who probably wouldn't have a shot at being drafted or getting to play professional ball make it through that door. It's so rewarding to see guys who have experienced success and then had a fall from grace and being there to help them recover and continue. To witness an athlete and his family's dreams come true after having worked their entire lives to achieve that dream and to be present to support them, to provide value through all their successes and failures. It reminds me how important we as a community are to one another. It gives me an intense sense of purpose when I see the impact my assistance and guidance have on the individuals I serve, and there's no other thing I'd rather be doing than providing a service that genuinely educates and empowers and helps mold young athletes into the leaders of tomorrow.

Q: What are your long-term goals as an agent?

A: My overall long-term goal as an agent is to change the industry radically. I would love to see the big operations gone; the large conglomerates, a thing of the past. I would like to see the industry evolve into a merit-based service and whoever provides the best service is the agency that has the clientele. My goal is to hang up my agent hat much earlier than many might assume because I think if I do my job well I should have a twenty-year career because the individuals I work with will be my replacement—I want to help mold my replacement. Another goal is a bit out of the realm of what I'm doing now, but in the sports school world, I'm an Ohio guy so I'd love to acquire one of my Ohio sports pro teams and know that my Buckeye State is well taken care of by bringing value to an organization. I make the most of the platform I'm on now, yet always aspire for a higher and new platform to take on.

Q: Is there anything about your current process as an agent that you would like to see changed or improved?

A: I think I'm getting better at it, but I tend to wear my heart on my sleeve. My transparency and honesty tend to make me feel vulnerable early on when I'm talking with a prospective client as opposed to waiting until after a couple of meetings to let them know the truth about the industry and about who I am as an agent and a man. I've concluded that if a prospective client dislikes my transparency and they walk away after meeting number one that's fine because I gave my best effort. My approach has been very successful, but I need to do it more frequently and more often in my process. And I think by leading with my transparency as opposed to waiting to build a certain level of connection I will increase the relationships tenfold.

Q: What advice would you give to other sports management students or law students who aspire to become agents?

A: Never stop. The thing about being an agent is that it doesn't matter what everyone else thinks about your motive for being an agent. Some might believe that it's about the money or that you're seeking the fame of a super-agent, or even that you love sports, but it boils down to the fact that you must believe you have a calling to do this work. The truth is: you are in this industry to solve a problem. I think that should be your goal in any business venture—how you solve the problem and how you go about solving the problem is the most exciting part of it all because that's going to be your journey. Just know that the journey is going to be extremely difficult. The most crucial advice that I heard at an agency in Chicago was, "You've got to keep going because many would-be advisors are going to *say* they want to do this work but very few are going to do the work." So continue to show up, do your best, and you will eventually make it, and that will look different for each person. Be persistent, knowing that this industry is a war of attrition, and that you will indeed receive your opportunity.

Q: What are some of the mental toughness tools you have used on your journey?

A: The primary mental toughness tool is embracing failure. If we are fearful of failure, we will never see success. By embracing and learning to love and appreciate and be critical of my failure I realize that it's actually not a failure at all. It's development. And so that was a mental toughness tool I had to sharpen because I realized that the only way to progress in life is through experience. I learned the term "carpe diem" in middle school, which means *seize the day*. To me it says that you keep going, you use your day to the fullest, maximize your opportunities because everyone's version of success exists in the world. But it's up to you to define it and to go get it. Leave it all on the field and/or court!

Part II
PROCESS

GOAL FIVE

Re-calculating the Process toward a Culture of Empowerment

"We cannot seek achievement for ourselves and forget about progress and prosperity for our community... Our ambitions must be broad enough to include the aspirations and needs of others, for their sakes and for our own."

~Cesar Chavez

This is an exciting stop on our journey toward becoming an empowered stakeholder. At this stop I'm going to show you exactly how to establish and grow a culture of empowerment which provides maximum opportunities for all.

First, as I've stated in previous chapters, education is the central key and focal point for every stakeholder involved in the athletic process. Now that you have a picture of the current landscape, and you understand how the current process works, you're ready for an environment where you can think creatively and make innovative decisions toward how the future is going to look. Being properly educated in the current process will impact how you conduct yourself moving forward.

I want to establish the fact that the current process isn't sustainable for the future and this is due to the fact that amateurism is going to be altered. I'm not saying that the NCAA is going away by any means, but, in the future, we're going to be moving toward a dynamic where

1. stakeholders are more educated on the process,
2. stakeholders possess a strong understanding of the business side, and
3. athletes realize that at the end of the day, getting an opportunity to attend college to play a sport is based on the value an athlete brings to the team and school.

But we want to then take it to the next level—playing professionally. You'll need to come at the situation knowing the value you bring to the table, and what opportunities you'll have as you work on increasing your value in specific areas. Areas for stakeholders include:

1. your specific value from a marketing standpoint,
2. your physical value as an athlete,
3. your knowledge value as a parent who's supporting your student-athlete in the decision-making process,
4. your value as a coach installing knowledge, and mentoring the individuals on your team,
5. your value as a team, understanding the ability to grow the value of your personnel and organization, and finally
6. your value as an industry professional to bring influence and positive change.

Shift in Sports Agency Model

Within the sports agency realm, the industry is moving toward agents acting more as business managers who can help athletes manage their life as a whole, not just the athletic aspects.

The business manager would fulfill several roles to help their athlete clients. The role of the business manager would include marketing consultant, helping the athlete grow their brand awareness and brand value. Another aspect would be a contractual developer, making sure the athlete has the most advantageous contract possible.

Your responsibility as an athlete within the process would be to ensure your value stays high in the physical and mental realm. Continued responsibility is sharpening each area, and also making sure practices are in place in order to thrive under the pressures you'll be facing as you navigate the process of achieving your goals, whether you're transitioning from high school to college, or college to pro.

The solution involves unpacking the truth that the process is undeniably moving toward a value-based process. The new process will embody recognizing your intrinsic and extrinsic value, amplifying it, and then finding ways to magnify the value of those around you. I call it Empowered Leadership. You may be asking at this point: *how will stakeholders gain the education to successfully navigate within an empowered leadership process?*

There should be some form of curriculum at each level— each level of curriculum needs to be managed by whoever has the most authority at that level. In Rashad McCants' trailblazing and controversial book, *Plantation Education — The Exploitation of the Modern-Day Athlete-Student*[1], he stresses the need to have academic advisors at schools who are uniquely skilled and trained to work with athletes as the process and academic steps look different than those of traditional students.

For the high school and travel ball level, there should be a coach or someone from the athletic department, a key figure who basically explains the dos and don'ts of what can and cannot be done on behalf of the athlete, the family, and the team itself. That individual would be in charge of educating you on how you should navigate, how the whole process collectively works. Same thing at the collegiate level; your education on

---

[1] McCants, Rashad, Plantation Education, The Exploitation of the Modern-Day Athlete-Student, New York: Post Hill Press, 2018.

the process would be someone in the administrative office at the university who has a vested interest in you thriving as an individual. On a professional level, the responsibility to educate should fall to the players unions and I think retired pro athletes would play a key role in the education process. Some education is already taking place but not nearly to the magnitude it should be.

Looking long term, the education sector could include a 4 to 6-week crash course, a boot camp of sorts that stakeholders attend prior to entering their specific athletic phase whether AAU, high school, college, or pro. It would be a module-type course provided by whoever has the most power and influence at that particular level.

Self-education is vital as well. An athlete, or any stakeholders for that matter, should not blindly listen to and follow instructions, no matter how "informed" the educator may seem, or how slick they appear. Do your homework. Research. Talk to people. You wouldn't have major surgery without asking the surgeon pertinent questions, would you? The same applies to your athletic experience. If you don't educate yourself, you could have a long recovery time if you make crucial mistakes in the process.

A new, empowered process would ensure that the individuals speaking to stakeholders have already navigated through the process themselves, or have already worked in the sports industry in some capacity and/or have other relevant education, skills, and/or experience.

In addition, those speaking to the stakeholders would actively pursue events where sports thought-leaders are the keynote speakers; that would place the educator in a prime position to glean inside industry information they can then pass on to the stakeholders. And any mode an individual can use to get closer to the inside of what's really going on, and understand the business, the better positioned everyone involved will be.

I'd like to add here that there is a dramatic need to create a more democratic process that gives all key stakeholders a seat at the table.

Athletic Business Institute

The creation of an athletic business institute would fulfill the need to educate virtually anyone who will listen on all the aspects of the sports business industry, no matter what level. Not an accredited university that's giving a degree in sports business, rather an institute for those who are interested in understanding all facets of the sports business and how it operates and how they can play a role to positively influence sports business from the grassroots to the professional level. Who better to lead courses than former athletes, coaches, and other team personnel; those who have served through the highs and lows of their sport.

McCants states, "There is a business for doctors, there's a business for lawyers, hell, there's even a business for business. There's business school, there's law school, and there's med school. There should be a sports school to serve as a whole new brand of education for athletes to allow us a new pathway to postgraduate courses."

I think anyone who has gone through the process, understands it, and is willing to give back, would be the ideal individual to instruct stakeholders. Not some lawyer or professor or teacher or accountant. Those who have served in the trenches would be most influential by abiding by the mentality of "once you climb the ladder of success, send it back down." Those who have served in the trenches would be the most relatable and can best deliver a curriculum that's structurally organized in a way where stakeholders are able to hear it, understand it, and apply it to their own life.

If that type of culture were the norm, it would take the sports business to a much higher level. Required certification of the instructors in their specific areas of expertise would bring an increased level of credibility. If the expertise is in the legal field, we would say he's an Athlete Institute legal advisor, not an attorney, but someone adept at discussing the legal landscape of the process. The same principle would apply to an Athlete Institute life coach, financial planner, recruitment specialist, or transition and post-sport employment expert.

The certified instructors have no skin the game in that they're not a business trying to "sell" the stakeholders on anything, they're not trying to play at some level, they're not a recruiter; they're purely unbiased professionals on a mission to keep the integrity of the process intact, and making sure those rising up in the process are following the rules and conducting themselves appropriately.

The bottom line of the Athletic Institute would be simple: Educate and empower the stakeholders. Athletic Institute advisors and personnel would act as neutral third parties who provide unbiased advice and guidance, not the status quo of college coaches, shoe brands and agents who currently have all the influence.

Now let's turn our attention to your market value as a stakeholder.

Understanding and applying your market value applies to what your specific goals are, and at what level you're seeking to aspire. Are you a young athlete? Young coach? Seasoned coach or executive? A parent-coach? The answer, in part, is going to be unique to each individual, but the bulk of your value is your output, your results. What level are you at now and what is your output at your current level?

Consider this: if you're a three-foot-four basketball player who is playing varsity ball, and you're utterly amazing on the court, and you're bringing high value to your high school team, yet everyone else perceives your value might be lower, how do you handle that? There will come a time, if your goal is to make it to the NBA, that you'll need to be unreservedly honest and compare yourself against those who are also doing what you want to do. Take time to consider your USP (Unique Selling Proposition) as they say in the marketing world. Ask yourself, what do I do better, and unlike anyone else? This applies to an athlete, a coach, a parent-coach, or an agent.

Determining your market value involves intrinsically deciding what you're willing to do to achieve your goals. That's something that no one can measure. No one can tell you how much effort you're going to have to put forth. Take a serious look at the individuals who are in the same walk of life as you, and make a mental list of the characteristics and traits that define them.

From an athlete's viewpoint, you would determine your market value through your athletic output and/or attention from college coaches, scouts, and teams. The ongoing goal of the maximization of your value is finding out ways to make yourself better, more valuable whether it's through an education platform, a mental strength platform, a fitness platform, or a nutrition platform.

In addition to the platforms just mentioned, no one can deny the star power that ignites when athletes align themselves with mega brands. Even when a situation goes awry, like when Novak Djokovic lost a tiebreaker to Roger Federer in the men's final at Wimbledon, and subsequently tried and failed to tear off his own shirt. A New York Times article[2] reported, "For most of those watching, it engendered great amusement, but for Uniqlo, the Japanese brand that made the tennis great's outfit, it was marketing gold." The bottom line is: don't underestimate your market value on all counts!

From a coach's viewpoint, you can determine your market value by attending special training, conducting your own research, having roundtable talks with other coaches, and coaching the "whole" athlete, not just the physical element.

From a parent's viewpoint, you can determine your market value by researching and reading articles about how other parents are successfully maneuvering their student-athlete's athletic journey, creating roundtable discussions with other parents, and learning how to provide healthy motivation for your student-athlete.

---

[2] Arthur, Rachel, "The Marketing Power of Sports Stars," www.nytimes.com, https://www.nytimes.com/2016/04/05/fashion/sports-athletes-marketing.html, (Accessed 9/12/2018).

From an industry professional viewpoint, you can determine your market value through continual industry education, by improving your emotional intelligence so you relate better to your clients, keeping your negotiation skills sharp, and enlisting an assistant's help to keep you organized.

A workinsports.com[3] article highlights how one can be successful in sports business. The article includes insightful tips like first define what success means to you, do some market research, employ creativity, identify your rivals, make social media your friend, and prepare to make sacrifices.

The author states, "To be successful in any industry, you must be willing to make sacrifices and this can come in a variety of forms: from missing out on some friends and family time, to saving that extra bit of money."

The primary markets heavily investing in innovative technology are D1, D2, and D3 colleges with youth, amateur and eSports also racing to the tech king throne. Pro leagues and D1 universities march to the tune of major bucks as they dig into their deep pockets to amuse, entertainment, and inform their peers, fans, and media constituents with the latest tech innovations. Athletes using technology can increase their speed and knowledge of the game with VR simulators and performance data analytics. They can tap into any number of apps and programs to keep themselves playing at peak performance.

---

[3] Workinsports.com, *Guest submission from Business Owner Mark Lawrence of 5 Star Tennis Holidays,* "How to Make Your Sports Business Successful" https://www.workinsports.com/blog/how-to-make-your-sports-business-successful/ (Accessed 8/31/2018).

Say you want to be a franchise owner someday. Knowing the innovative changes rapidly taking place in the sports industry will keep you cutting edge when it comes to technology.

An article in verizonventures.com[4] states, "Clubs, leagues, players, media companies, colleges and even high schools are investing in technology to engage fans, enhance athlete performance and make participation in sports more fun. Intel CEO Brian Krzanich was spot on when he said 'consumers are choosing experiences over products.'"

Consider how the super-imposed yellow first down markers on NFL fields revolutionized how we watch the game. According a 2017 fastcompany.com[5] article, "This was the first mass-market implementation of augmented-reality technology, which places digitized visual information into real-world situations. The [sports industry] is on the front lines of where technology and culture collide. It's a collision that won't hurt your head, but it will encourage change."

---

[4] Heitlinger, Paul. "The Race for Innovation in Sports Tech." Verizonventures.com. http://www.verizonventures.com/blog/2017/09/the-race-for-innovation-in-sports-tech/ (Accessed 9/8/2018).

[5] Fast Company. "How the Sports Business Pioneered Advances in the Innovation Economy" fastcompany.com. https://www.fastcompany.com/3068298/how-the-sports-industry-pioneered-advances-in-the-innovation-econo (Accessed 9/1/2018).

Major League Baseball and NASCAR followed suit with their own technological innovations to keep fans more engaged. A 2014 article out of Stanford[6] stresses that CEOs wish they had "fans" instead of customers.

The article states, "While fan passion is as old as sport itself, leagues and franchises are now using cutting-edge technology not just to build winning teams but also to capitalize on the ardor of their customer base to grow another revenue source—corporate sponsorships."

Although the terms "fan" and "customer" are interchangeable in a plethora of ways, the fact remains the same: innovation is moving at lightning speed, and as a stakeholder, to keep relevant and retain and grow your value, you must keep up with the trends. From intuitive "smart" arenas to initializing greater fan engagement through YouTube game recaps to accelerating global programs for the NFL and NBA, keeping abreast of the latest technology is imperative for any stakeholder if you want a place in the behemoth called the sports industry.

In the past several years we've seen the rise of the CDO; chief digital officer and chief data officer. According to Wikipedia, "A Chief Data Officer is responsible for determining what kinds of information the enterprise will choose to capture, retain and exploit and for what purposes. A Chief Digital Officer often does not bear that business responsibility, but

---

[6] Mooney, Loren, with additional reporting by Natalie White. www.gsb.stanford.edu. "Five Key Trends That Are Driving the Business of Sports." https://www.gsb.stanford.edu/insights/five-key-trends-are-driving-business-sports

rather is responsible for the information systems through which data is stored and processed."

Understanding how technology is being infused into the sport experience brings us to how the Athlete Institute will operate.

An effusively technologically-advanced and ultra-innovative Athlete Institute would function as a resource to help you reach your full market value, because at the end of the day, your value is determined based on what you do and who you are. Your application of the knowledge and skills you're attaining will serve to continually increase your market value, thus making you a "brand" that teams will want to invest in. You must remain conscious of the process at play. If you respect and appreciate and learn to enjoy the process, and not fight it, not resist it, and not turn a blind eye to it, that's how you reap the most benefit.

Sheer Entertainment

The sheer entertainment value of sports should not be on the list of the most important components of an empowered process. What we as stakeholders must be concerned about is how we use the process to obtain value, leverage, and improve humanity. Fans who turn on their TVs for the games, get their tickets, go to the games, and buy jerseys, hats, and other paraphernalia are engaged, yet typically don't take that engagement beyond the game. We see idolized athletes because the fans allow them to be idolized. So let's not tell the athletes to shut up and dribble, to entertain us, then tell them to go home. Let's allow them to be stewards of the athletic chain. Allow them to be leaders in our community so they can effect positive change, and as exciting as it is to see an athlete hit a half-court shot, or throw or catch a Hail Mary pass, it's much more exciting to see them lean in and help others behind them get to that place in terms of whatever their definition of success looks like. They can do this by emulating the characteristics that helped them get to the top of their game. It's not just all about pushups and running. It's mental.

A culture of empowerment warrants a three-pronged solution:

1. **Sports Empowerment Institute** (SEI) (go-to, centralized education, empowerment, and innovation resource for all stakeholders)

2. **Empowered Mentorship** (one-on-one: retired players, coaches, and industry professionals mentoring current athletes on the conveyor belt, parents, coaches coming up in the process, and aspiring industry professionals)

3. **Annual Empowered Athlete Summit** (industry thought-leader speakers, breakout sessions for intensive interaction, focused education, and interactive empowerment)

Focus on Mentoring

All three solutions involve a collaborative approach but until the Sports Empowerment Institute is fully functional and the Empowered Athlete Summit is operational, we can start with mentoring because it's a quick solution we can enact today, even on an informal basis.

Mentoring can include teaching, coaching, advising, counseling, educating, tutoring, guiding, training, developing, molding, supporting, and shaping. Make it a point to find someone this week who's coming up in the current athletic process and agree to meet with them once a week; ideally in person, although Skype or Zoom can serve as a more personal alternative.

Where do you find such a person? Look on your social media sites like LinkedIn, Facebook, Instagram, or Twitter. Look for the *hungry* athlete, "green" coach, parent, or rookie agent. Set a few parameters for your meetings, and prepare a loose agenda although you'll want to be open to any topics or challenges your mentee wants to discuss.

In Dru Joyce's book, *Beyond championships: A Playbook for Winning at Life*, LeBron James acknowledges Joyce as the person who taught him not only about basketball but about life. Joyce was LeBron's high school basketball coach and his mentoring helped LeBron manage challenges on and off the court as well as how to navigate through life in general.

An insightful article on the National Mentoring Resource Center website[7] states, "The legendary Boston Celtic Bill Russell once said, 'If you ask any NBA player, executive, or coach about their path to success, on and off the court, you'll quickly see the same pattern emerge. None of us made it on our own.' Russell himself benefited from mentoring; if it were not for Russell's junior high basketball coach he would

---

[7] Roulier, Rebekah, LMHC, Associate Director of Doc Wayne Youth Services. "Mentoring At-Risk Youth Through the Power of Sports." https://nationalmentoringresourcecenter.org/index.php/nmrc-blog/142-mentoring-at-risk-youth-through-the-power-of-sports.html (Accessed 9/18/2018).

not have even continued on with the sport. Likely, you are not mentoring a professional athlete, but you may be able to harness the power of sport to impact a child's life."

Mentoring is certainly not reserved for the able-bodied. *Sport for Community* was designed to empower people with disabilities and promote rights and inclusion worldwide. One post on state.gov[8] states, "Every April 6th people around the globe come together to celebrate the United Nations International Day of Sport for Development and Peace… Every day, the State Department's Sports Diplomacy division harnesses that power to bring people together through programs including Sports Envoy, Sports Grants, and the latest addition to the family, *Sport for Community*: Global Sports Mentoring Program on disability rights."

In 2017, Sport for Community welcomed sixteen international emerging leaders in the disability sports sector to the United States for a mentorship exchange at top American adaptive sports organizations.

Iresearchnet.com[9] adds to the mix, "Research conducted across diverse settings and individuals has shown that mentoring works and leads to such positive outcomes such as higher performance, faster career advancement, positive

---

[8] Arnold, Nation. "International Athletes and American Mentors Change the World Through 'Sport for Community.'" https://blogs.state.gov/stories/2017/04/06/en/international-athletes-and-american-mentors-change-world-through-sport (Accessed 9/18/2018).

[9] IRE Search Net. "Mentoring in Sport." Iresearchnet.com http://psychology.iresearchnet.com/sports-psychology/psychological-skills/mentoring-in-sport/ (Accessed 9/17/2018).

emotional states, and psychological growth and development. Mentoring effects are robust, having been shown to be effective in a variety of educational, sport, and business settings as well as in the field of positive youth development."

The article goes on to say that one year to eighteen months is the optimal length for effective mentoring and a minimum of four hours a month is the necessary commitment. A mentor should focus on screening a mentee to ensure they are ready for mentoring, and are serious about their commitment before beginning the formal training. A mentor should cultivate and maintain their relationship with the mentee to gain trust, an essential ingredient for any successful mentorship, and actually must be present for both parties to establish a meaningful ongoing mentoring relationship. There will come a time when the mentor and mentee will decide to part ways or terminate the relationship and that needs to be defined as well. Perhaps retooling the nature of the relationship is discussed, as is defining any and all future communication. A mentoring relationship can be fulfilling on both sides but most often is most rewarding for the mentor as you observe the mentee putting your insight and advice into action and seeing tangible results. Be prepared to reap abundant benefits!

In the Q & A session for Chapter Five, listen to what Jalen Washington has to say about his own journey coming up as a college athlete and progressing in a professional baseball league. Up and coming athletes will want to pay careful attention to Jalen's journey.

Intersection of Education and Empowerment

Direction Questions:

What are you doing on an ongoing basis to maximize your value as a stakeholder?

Are you investing yourself in education? Mentorship? Sports performance coach? Nutritional specialist? Mental strength coach?

Empowerment Exercise:

1. Make a list of all the tools (skills) of your trade that you do not currently possess and make it your daily objective to do at least one thing to obtain those skills and abilities.

2. For those skills that you already possess, learn one new thing daily and look for ways to use your skills to elevate others.

3. If you don't have a current mentor, start actively searching for one. Don't be afraid to interview a few to find the right fit for you.

Q & A Session

Jalen Washington
San Diego Padres Organization
Catcher, Fielder, First Baseman

Q: Tell us a little about your sports background.

A: I grew up playing baseball, basketball and football through high school. Wasn't exactly sure what my favorite was but I was given a couple of opportunities for each sport, and ultimately made the decision to play baseball at Ohio State where I played all four years. I played a little bit of infield, and I also played catcher. Playing both positions provided me with the diversity that helped me get drafted. This past season was my first full season with the Padres.

Q: How long had you been looking for an advisor before meeting Michael McGinnis?

A: I had been looking casually for a few months because other athletes around me were getting agents. But when I met Michael I knew he was the right guy for me; I felt like he understood my situation and was going to help me and push me and get my name out there. I felt like he would provide the impetus for me to get drafted, and then be successful during and after my sports career.

Q: Describe a frustration or a challenge you experienced while even casually searching for an advisor.

A: The frustration was that some of the athletes around me were finding agents at the time and agents weren't reaching out to me even though I felt like my athletic talent was on par with other athletes at my level. I kept wondering, *Why aren't they reaching out and talking to me?* It was at this point I realized that baseball is a business and if I wanted to excel, I would need an advisor to guide me.

Q: Who was involved in the decision-making process for finding an advisor?

A: It was my parents and me. I also reached out to some teammates who had agents at the time and then some of my coaches. I reached out to my coaches because most if not all of them had played pro ball and they had experience with finding agents and going through agencies. Their advice was to find a person with whom I worked well with and not just someone who had a big name. The coaches added that the smaller agencies would take care of me on a more personal level, which is what I found with Michael.

Q: What criteria did you use for finding an agent, and what were your deal-breakers?

A: It was my senior year, the beginning of the baseball season, and Michael approached me with a phone call. At the time I wasn't looking for an agent, but he provided some valuable information about some things, the things that I really wanted. And then I got a chance to sit down and meet with him. Michael was representing one of my teammates at the time, so we all got together in Arizona to talk. I fired a whole bunch of questions at him; questions that both my parents and I had, because I wasn't very familiar with having an agent, what the process was, and he broke it down and made it simple to understand. I liked what I heard, so it was an easy choice.

Q: How long have you been a client of Michael's?

A: In an official capacity, once I got drafted, but he was more of an advisor when I was in college, so probably the third week into my senior year is when I started talking to him. He advised me a lot and helped me understand the process while I was still playing college, and we made it official when I finally signed a pro contract.

Q: Much of an agent's role is to educate you when you're first going through the process; what to expect, how to navigate. What exceptional qualities stood out in Michael that caused you to choose him as your agent?

A: He was very personable, and he wasn't talking just to talk, he was more of an educator. He made sure I understood what he was trying to do for me and what he could do for me. The first time we met, he was fine with me saying no to him, backing away and going in a different direction. His goal was to make sure I understood what the process was and how he could help me out in my future. The one thing that got me was when he said, "If you go with me or not, if you need someone to talk to or need help or advice with anything, you can always reach out to me. Life goes further than baseball and if baseball doesn't work out and you need help finding a job, I can help you out." It was obvious that Michael was someone who looks at his role as more than just making money off of athletes and their parents. He went a step beyond what I even knew I was looking for, so that's what was great about him.

Q: What has your experience been like working with a sports agent/advisor?

A: It's been good. Michael reaches out to me probably once every two weeks. It's not too much, but I know he's still there. He's helping me just because he wants to help me; that's part of who Michael is.

Q: What results have you experienced since working with Michael? What has he done for you?

A: He's been someone who I can talk to besides my teammates or parents about how the process is going because he understands that baseball has a long season and there are a lot of ups and downs. He's always been a positive vibe. When I talk to him, I know he's going to give it to me straight, but he's also going to give me the truth and provide something positive that I can take from the situation. He's helped me out financially with gear and bats, and he also works hard helping me in the off-season. He's trying to get me to work at baseball camps with kids who are looking for a mentor or a coach so I can make a little money. We've been trying to put something together for a couple of months now, and I can't thank him enough for the education and insight he's providing.

Q: What are your short- and long-term sports goals, and how do you envision Michael helping you achieve them?

A: Obviously, the long-term goal is to make it to the big leagues. And by Michael doing what he's doing right now is more than enough for me, because people who are there when you're not as important are the people you keep around when you finally make it because there are plenty of bandwagoners out there who want to hitch their wagon to your star when you make it big. My short-term goal is to continue to move up the minor league system every year, and to better myself along the way. It's a hard and tough system to move up in, and there's a lot of grinding that goes on, but I'll keep at it until I make it.

Q: Are you open to any team in the major leagues, or would you like to stay with the Padres?

A: The primary goal is to make it to the big leagues no matter what team. I'm thankful for the Padres and everything they've done for me, and I hope that it's in a Padres uniform when I finally get there, but in the end, the goal is to make it, whatever team that is.

Q: Is there anything about Michael as an agent that you would like to see changed or improved?

A: One thing we've talked about is working to get better connections. Because Michael is relatively new to the sports agent game, he works very hard at making connections and expanding his network so he can reach out to some of the sports equipment companies to get bats and batting gloves. As he develops his network, we'll all win.

Q: What advice would you give to other young athletes looking for an agent?

A: Find the person or agency who's right for you, and don't just find an agent to say you have an agent. Do your homework. Do your research. Make sure everything the agent tells you is going to happen actually happens, because the easy part is talking a big game *before* you sign, but it's your job to make sure they're following through on the things they promised you *after* you sign.

Q: What are your go-to mental strength tools that you've used in the process of being an athlete and wanting to rise in the ranks?

A: Mental toughness is one of those things that's kind of on the rise right now. A lot more teams and a lot more athletes are using it. The biggest one for me is visualization and having an understanding of my goals and what I want to do. I'm a firm believer in that if you visualize success and visualize where you want to be, that your actions will follow what you're envisioning. And at the end of the day, you'll be happy with what you did to reach that goal.

GOAL SIX

Implementing the New Process to Reach Your Destination!

"Day by day, what you choose, what you think and what you do is who you become."

~Heraclitus

In recent years we have witnessed a dreadful lack of active engagement and participation in sports. The NFL is a classic example. There's so much drama and controversy surrounding the new national anthem regulations. Fans are fed up. Athletes are fed up. Teams and leagues are fed up. Industry sports professionals are fed up. If things continue this way, it will undoubtedly lead to lost revenue and failing businesses, which doesn't benefit anyone involved.

Creating a process that embodies empowerment, accountability, mentorship, innovation, and collaboration will create abundant opportunities and industries. This type of empowered approach will improve the current process while radically increasing the value everyone reaps. This is the future of sports. As we saw in Chapter Five, the sports industry desperately needs a new way forward, and a new way to deal with individuals caught in the cogs of greed, selfishness, and the imbalance of power. In the sports industry it's easy to develop mistrust by the *me-first, money-first* mentality where everyone thinks you want to take something from them. You're looked at sideways when you come to fill someone's pot; but one thing is certain: filling another's pot will eventually fill yours.

Now we're going to break down this section into distinctive pros and cons of the current process.

Pros of the Current Process:

Pro #1: Financial outlook is promising — Sports leagues, particularly in the United States, are generating billions in revenue. Everyone likes to argue that some athletes make millions of dollars, but sports teams are valued in the billions of dollars which makes the millions pale in comparison.

Pro #2: Provides an outlet to people — The current process provides opportunities that would not otherwise exist if it were not for their physical skills and/or attributes.

Pro #3: Opportunity for growth — The current sports business landscape provides stakeholders the opportunity to better themselves as individuals and allows them to grow through smart work and sacrifice.

Cons of the Current Process:

Con #1: Focus is on competition and not collaboration. Yes, there is and should be fierce competition in sports but this is also not gladiatorial combat. Losing in sports and/or sports business should provide value and growth and that's only possible through collaboration within the inner workings of the industry.

Con #2: Power is not evenly distributed. Each stakeholder should have a seat at the table and a voice in the decision-making process as well as some level of authority.

Con #3: Regulations are not keeping up with the rate of change. As the industry and the world continue to change at a rapid pace, the regulations that determine how the process runs need to be continuously evolving to keep up with the change. They need to be fluid and allow for change.

ଊ   ଈ

I see the Solution as a (United Nations) UN-type body, made entirely up of key stakeholders (parents, players, coaches, schools, teams, and sports industry professionals) with one to three representatives from each stakeholder group who vote and voice their views and opinions about their constituents. The Solution's motto would be something similar to: **A voice for all. Solutions for all**. It would include a non-binding advisor to guide the sports industry from grassroots to pro influence. The Solution must start earlier in the process and expand opportunities to larger populations. Through leaning on the benefits of a nonprofit and focusing on grassroots, regional, national, and eventually, having a global impact, collaboratively, we'll learn how to get the process right and have the most positive impact.

Although it's more effective than the current process, the Solution also has positives and negatives. It's positive because it brings people together. Everyone needs to understand and realize we are all interconnected. What happens to *any* human being, happens to *every* human being. If people don't realize this, they're not going to buy in, which makes it harder to advance the idea. Envision players and even fans becoming shareholders—especially with extremely profitable businesses. Although savvy business people created this behemoth, the downside is that it really only benefits a small percentage of individuals; those with the ownership stake.

Similar to how some corporations allow employees to become shareholders, I think players, and even fans, should have some equity stake in these organizations because they too should also have the ability to enjoy some of the power and influence. Obviously the logistical details would require a lot of thought and reflection, so it's not going to happen tomorrow. However, in order for change to occur there must be a call to action, as well as bringing new ideas and plans to consider.

Change will require stakeholders to see the vision, and athletes will probably be the first to initiate it. They are ultimate leaders and the reason the industries even exist. The change will occur once they realize they are interconnected. This collaboration between athletes will create a positive ripple effect throughout the industry. Disputes like lockouts will be a thing of the past. Once the Solution is in full effect it will create a win-win dynamic. The goal for athletes is to educate, empower, and hold themselves accountable so that we all find a middle ground — and finding the middle ground is the best form of negotiation because we're able to give and receive simultaneously.

Colin Kaepernick can be seen in history as a unifying act as opposed to the divisive trendsetter those in Washington and the media are making him out to be. We must take a step back to remember that Kaepernick was actually protesting police brutality and other social injustice, *not* the national anthem or "the troops" as some in our government leadership have suggested.

My objective is that the Solution becomes the status quo for making agreements, putting together deals, and resolving disputes. I hope, globally, that this is the wave rolling in a new era.

The Solution would go far beyond sports to corporations, brands, church groups, buddies playing video games, etc. Through collaboration we can solve any problem. To be clear, I'm not advocating getting rid of competition. I'm trying to make competition fun. Competition is distorted when we're competing for our benefit and someone else's detriment. But if we take a collaborative approach, everyone thrives together. That's the aim, but how do we get the skeptics on board?

As with anything, there are always going to be naysayers, but the aim is to make them *yea-sayers*. Skeptics might argue that an environment where everyone wins will never work. I'd counter by telling them to try it, let the process unfold. They will see the value applied to young athletes' lives. For example, they might see a practice squad player secure a marketing deal. He's getting an opportunity that's usually given to the star quarterback. Other athletes will see that understanding their market value exponentially increases their opportunities. They will undoubtedly be inspired by the practice player and strive for similar results.

The Solution is not aimed at furthering the "everybody gets a trophy" culture, as that mentality is also problematic, but rather is focused on the true value an individual has and brings to the table, and receiving fair compensation and recognition for their unique value. Non-believers will start believing in the process after witnessing athletes evolve into better versions of themselves personally, professionally, and athletically.

On a personal level, athletes will be more at peace with themselves. They will be able to employ practices that make them happy. For example, athletes like Jalen Washington can use their visualization techniques for personal success as well as professional success to create a content, fulfilled life overall. Or like Curtis Madden, former college athlete and father of a current NFL player, who revels in who his son is, not what he does on the field. Now *that's* being at peace with oneself! Curtis doesn't gush about his son playing the in NFL, he loves and supports his son because of his sonship, not his position in life.

Professionally, athletes will have opportunities to receive their fair value because the empowered approach creates a heightened self-awareness. Everyone understands who they are, what they are doing, what they're about, and what they aspire to be. Being conscious of these things and working to improve them will yield financial returns in an athlete's professional career. The following examples provide a snapshot of what pro leagues are doing to empower their athletes.

1. The Wharton Business School for NFL athletes is a nicely put together model that reveals opportunities are out there to be grabbed, and shows a willingness of the NFL to educate.

2. The Wharton Sports Business Academy[1] "teaches students about ownership, sports agents, marketing, media, and labor as they meet and learn from leaders in the sports business world. The program examines various academic disciplines as they apply to the sports industry with an overview of the business and

---

[1] Wharton Sports Business Initiative. "Wharton Sports Business Academy." https://wsb.wharton.upenn.edu/students/wharton-sports-business-academy/. (Accessed 9/8/2018).

legal aspects of various intercollegiate, Olympic and professional sports enterprises."

3. In 2012 we witnessed NFL Player Engagement and the Wharton Sports Business Initiative announce the maiden voyage of the NFL-Wharton Prep Leadership Program[2]. The Prep Leadership Program was designed as a "highly selective leadership and achievement recognition program for a select group of elite male and female student-athletes. The program recognizes the success of the invitees both on the field and in the classroom and provides participants with two days of specific leadership training and development programming." Instructors include top faculty from Wharton and the NFL, and focus on such topics as Basics of Leadership, Professional Development, Career Development, Financial Education, and Basic of Management. The NFL-Wharton Prep Leadership Program states, "The rigorous coursework, breakout groups, and panels specifically designed by the NFL and Wharton will provide a formal foundation of leadership training for the next generation of leaders."

4. In 2015 we saw the inaugural NFL Prep Academy[3] at University of Pennsylvania, an invitation-only program designed for elite high school football student-athletes and their parent or guardian to teach the values of education, character, leadership, and

---
[2] NFL Player Engagement. "Introducing the NFL-Wharton Prep Leadership Program." http://www.nflplayerengagement.com/prep/articles/introducing-the-nfl-wharton-prep-leadership-program/ (Accessed 9/13/2018).
[3] Pro Football Hall of Fame. "Pro Football Hall of Fame to Host Inaugural NFL Prep Academy." http://www.profootballhof.com/news/pro-football-hall-of-fame-to-host-inaugural-nfl-prep-academy/ (Accessed 9/13/2018).

community outreach. The four-day program features a variety of classroom presentations that include "Goal Setting," "Values," "Academic and Career Planning," "Healthy Relationships," "Life Beyond Football" and "Leadership & Character Development."

5. The Soccer Institute demonstrates how the education model can be applied to certain aspects of the industry on a micro level. A handful of educational institutions are doing a good job of equipping future sports professionals.

6. The Sports Business Institute (SBI)[4] is a private learning institution based in Barcelona, Spain with a regional office in Miami, USA, that provides top-quality practical executive business training to those aspiring to work or advance their career in sports, with a particular focus on the football/soccer industry. According to SBI, "Our programs have been designed to bridge the gap between an academic approach to sports management and the real-life work environment of the industry."

7. Kutztown University's (Berks County, Pennsylvania) Department of Sport Management and Leadership Studies[5] supports their mission by providing their students with "exceptional educational opportunities" by preparing "Sport Management majors to be leaders and contributors in the sport industry, preparing university students to make healthy decisions

---

[4] Sports Business Institute. http://www.sbibarcelona.com. http://www.sbibarcelona.com/about-sbi. (Accessed 9/13/2018).
[5] Kutztown University. www.kutztown.edu. https://www.kutztown.edu/about-ku/mission-vision-and-purpose.htm. (Accessed 9/13/2018).

throughout their lives, and by preparing university students for leadership and entrepreneurship opportunities."

As you can see by the examples above, institutions are indeed making an impact when it comes to increasing an athlete's market value through education and leadership training. When an athlete is empowered on one level it causes a trickle-down effect into all areas of their performance.

Athletically speaking, athletes will see their performance increase because they will be more receptive to self-evaluation and criticism. For example, maybe an athlete is great on offense, but the process shows them they need more development on defense. Later they work on it with coaches, staff, and teammates, and soon they are playing offense and defense equally well. By being conscious of who they are and where they want to go, their athletic performance improves through empowerment, education, and collaboration.

Intersection of Education and Empowerment

Direction Questions:

Who are YOU as an individual? Hint: You're not your name, your status, your ability, or your education. Who ARE you?

Are you doing your part to create an empowered sports system?

What do you aspire to be within the sports system?

Empowerment Exercise:

Do an online search for an educational workshop or course you can take to increase your knowledge of the sports industry, no matter where you lie as a stakeholder.

Make a list of people you'd like to collaborate with in the sports industry. Send one email, make one call. Daily.

Part III
SUCCESS

GOAL SEVEN

The Empowered Mindset Routes to Success

"Try not to become a man of success, but rather try to become a man of value."

~Albert Einstein

It's a given that during an athlete's journey he'll need an abundance of mental toughness to reach the pinnacle of success. We're familiar with the term *it takes a village to raise a child*...yet that same term also applies to the sports world. It's not only athletes who need mental strength, it's also those around them; the other stakeholders who encourage, support, and keep the athlete accountable. In this chapter I'll discuss how all stakeholders can maintain mental strength during the sports journey, especially after their playing days are over, no matter if those playing days are as an athlete, parent, coach, agent, or other sport professional.

An empowered mindset is embracing a mental edge that leaps over average, runs past mediocre, and crosses the finish line of mental toughness. An article entitled *It's All in Their Heads: The Mental Edge of Athletes Who Win*[1] states, "Being mentally tough means that no matter how brutal the circumstances—whether it's your 14th hour running through a desert in temperatures well over 100F or you're halfway through a 400-rep workout that includes pull-ups and single-leg squats—you're able to withstand the pain and suffering and perform to the best of your skills and talents, with a good time, high place, or even a win."

As I said, if you're not an athlete but rather one who is surrounding the athlete, these characteristics apply to you too. You may not be running through a 100-degree desert but you could be facing a tough personal or family challenge. You may not have the strength to endure a 400-rep workout but you are facing a devastating health or financial setback.

---

[1] Tamarkin, Sally. "It's All in Their Heads: The Mental Edge of Athletes Who Win." greatest.com. https://greatist.com/fitness/mental-training-tips-professional-athletes (Accessed 9/19/2018).

That same mental strength an athlete must summon to move past hurdles and pain, you must too!

In his provocative book, *Legacy*[2], James Kerr details fifteen life lessons from the New Zealand All Blacks. In one passage Kerr states, "There is a saying: 'There are no crowds lining the extra mile.' On the extra mile, we are on our own: just us and the road, just us and the blank sheet of paper, just us and the challenge we've set ourselves. It's the work we do behind closed doors that makes the difference out on the field of play, in whichever field we compete, whether we're in a team, leading a business or just leading our life."

His point? "Champions do extra." Developing mental toughness is doing extra.

There are certain qualities of the mentally tough that differentiate them from those who collapse when the pressure is on. Here are a few I've identified:

The mentally tough...

Remain calm under pressure. Getting a bit nervous before or during a major challenge is normal but you are still in full control and you do not allow your nervousness to distract you.

Are undaunted by competition and conditions. You do not falter in the face of bigger, stronger competitors. In fact, they motivate you even further to excel and exceed.

---

[2] Kerr, James, Legacy 15 Lessons in Leadership, London: (Constable, 2013). Pg. 134.

Exhibit a winning attitude no matter what. You are always on time or early for meetings. You outwork everyone else. You listen to your superiors and are not afraid to make adjustments to your game to become smarter and more efficient in your tasks. You have the heart of a champion!

Stay fully present in the moment. You don't dwell on haters or negative comments. You don't have time to marinate in past failures. Your amazing powers of concentration allow you to focus on the task at hand and tune out everything else.

Are perpetual learners. You do not ignore good advice. You seek to learn from mentors, teachers, and other successful people in your field. You read books and watch motivational videos to keep your edge sharp.

Possess an unwavering belief in themselves. You know without a shadow of a doubt that you can do this! Disappointments do not shake your belief in yourself, or your dreams. You are resilient and rebound quickly from losses and setbacks. When you get knocked down, you quickly refocus on improving your skills and performing better going forward.

Now, let's engage 10 critical action steps to unlock your mental kingdom:

1. **Employ mindfulness practices on a daily basis.** Practicing mindfulness involves accepting whatever arises in your awareness at each moment. It involves being kind and forgiving toward yourself. Mindfulness involves staying in the present

and not obsessing about the past or the future. It's noticing the sensory aspects of your body; sight, touch, smell, taste and sound so that you savor every sensation.

2. **Implement a daily habit of journaling and meditation.** I often think of the Kareem Abdul-Jabbar quote, "What the mind thinks, the body does," which is a key part of mental strength. There are a few very honest, transparent, mindful practices that I'm consistently employing in my own life in the way of journaling and meditation, and I just know how powerful the mental aspect is, and how transformative that can be.

There are journaling and meditation apps on your phone you can use to make it quick and easy. You don't have to be a Pulitzer Prize winner to write a few lines in a journal about what you're feeling, what challenges you're experiencing, or what successes you've had. As far as meditation, if you aren't currently practicing meditation, start with five minutes (set a timer) and build from there. It doesn't have to be a wooooo-wooooo experience. Just sit quietly for several minutes and let go of outside thoughts and stresses. This can work wonders for your mental strength.

3. **Understand, love, respect, and appreciate yourself for who and how you are.** No one on earth is exactly like you. No one has your exact DNA. No one else on the planet executes your skills and talents precisely the way you do.

4. **Recognize your own human nature**. Once you're able to realize your own human nature, it makes it far easier to recognize it in your brother, your wife, your co-worker, your supervisor, because then you're able to realize *wow, that's just human reaction. That's just a human response*. We are all prone to stress, excitement, sadness, or anger; it's called being human. Give yourself a break, and give others a break.

   David Cameron Gikandi, in his book Happy Pocket Full of Money[3], calls our self-perception and circumstances "jackets." He says, "…you are not some of the things you have all along thought you were. These "jackets" are helpful and useful, but sometimes they can hold you back. People who identify too much with their jackets, especially negative ones, place themselves in a prison, a box, a position from which they are unable to escape for fear that their self will be violated, or that their self is not capable, while all along it isn't their true Self. The next time you catch yourself saying "I can't do that because I am…" reexamine the "I am" bit and ask yourself whether that is really you or a jacket you picked up along the way, a jacket that you know for sure you will one day take off, a jacket that you may as well take off now."

5. **Practice authenticity**. Striving to keep up with the Joneses isn't our authentic self. Authenticity helps you feel comfortable with yourself, comfortable in your own skin. It's critical that you embrace and appreciate

---

[3] David Cameron Gikandi, *Happy Pocket Full of Money*, (Virginia, Hampton Roads, 2011), 196.

your uniqueness. Remember, no one else on the planet has your fingerprints!

6. **Choose empowering, positive reading material, and listen to motivational podcasts**. Inundate yourself with morning and nighttime messages that build you up. With YouTube, Audible, and all the other tools at our fingertips, we can download positivity into our brains in one click.

7. **Choose empowering, positive people to spend time with**. Think of the people in your life who tell you that you *can* do it, you *can* make it, you *can*, you *can*, you *can*. The people who truly care about you will speak growth and maturity into your life by telling you that you can become a greater version of yourself by doing X, Y and Z.

8. **Stay away as much as possible from negative, verbally-destructive, energy-vampires who often pose as friends, family, acquaintances…and sometimes yourself; your inner-me**. Certain people in our lives, and we know who they are, seem to be specifically designed to zap our self-confidence, sending constant overt and covert messages that you're not good enough, tall enough, fast enough, smart enough.

9. **Call out the greatness in others**. The motivational master, Zig Ziglar, once said, "You can get everything you want out of life by helping others get what they want." He and other motivational greats like Jim Rohn, Les Brown, Wayne Dyer, Eric Thomas, and Tony

Robbins have made it their life's mission to provide empowering messages to anyone who will listen. Piggyback onto their messages to speak greatness into others' lives. Yours will be enriched in the process!

10. **Get Your Financial House in Order.** You may think that finances have nothing to do with mental strength but you'd be wrong. They have *everything* to do with how you see yourself in all areas of your life. Building wealth is making your money work for you instead of you working for your money.

Gikandi puts it like this, "Wealthy people take a portion of their income from each day and put it into investments that grow on their own, automatically and without further work, over a long-term period. That way, a portion of each day that you work for money, that money ends up working for you for many years to come. That is a major key to wealth—getting a percentage of your income every day to work for you without your intervention."

Nothing will empower you more than knowing how to build and sustain wealth.

☙   ❧

You have to get to a point where even though the world around you is saying go left, you possess enough self-confidence within yourself to go right. Not to sound overly religious but that thought reminds me of Jesus. He didn't hang around with all the saints and noble people. He hung around with sinners. People who were *less than* in the eyes of others.

And Jesus was no wimp. He loved, he taught, he corrected, but he wasn't a pushover in any sense of the word. When people begged him and tugged on his robe with multitudes surrounding him, He addressed the issues that needed to be addressed, and He had righteous anger when he needed it. He led by example and did not merely follow the ways of the majority.

Likewise, my ambition isn't to hang around a bunch of hoity-toity billionaires and say, *Hey, I want to be like you*. No change will come from that. Change only comes from meeting people where they are and showing them where they can go. I want to go hang around a bunch of people who are disenfranchised, and bring my light to them so their light can shine through mine.

Go to places where you're needed most and help that group shine, help them understand the potential in their life. Establish enough mental strength and fortitude to be who you are, and from there, you can take what you own mentally and nourish that same empowerment in the lives of other people, because that's the crux of leading by example, which is always my favorite course of action. I don't care for lip service. I just want to see what you're going to do.

Drive and Mental Resolve

A famous quote says, *what the mind thinks, the body does*. Drive and mental resolve are the keys that can turn our mental engine into understanding that what you want to obtain is only possible through what you're willing to do and/or let go of to get to your destination.

Say it out loud: *what the mind thinks, the body does.* Drive comes from the recognition that nothing's going to fall into your lap. Nothing's going to magically happen. No stardust. No magic fairy. You have to want it, you have to be hungry, you have to be ambitious, and you have to be willing to push, pull, and do anything it takes to get to your desired destination. Drive means doing what you have to do even when it's uncomfortable, when no one's watching, when you're tired, when you're sick. You still have to show up. You still have to perform. You still have to produce.

Mental fortitude means accepting your limitations but not conceding to those limitations. You may think, *yeah, I may have this ankle injury, but I'm not going to let it stop me from doing what I need to do.* That's the kind of strength that says I have to achieve a task, and it will be achieved no matter how I feel in this exact moment, because this is what I'm called upon to do. Practicing mental fortitude is another way of leading by example. It's showing others how to conduct themselves. This concept applies to all stakeholders in the athletic process, not just the athlete.

Limited Mindset vs Limitless Mindset

The opposite of mental strength is having a scarcity mentality. A scarcity mentality says that you'll never have enough, be enough, do enough to be successful and that's a no-win situation because you'll always fall short. When you get yourself out of this thinking sinkhole, and eliminate the word *can't* from your vocabulary, there is no limit on success.

There is a vast difference between a **limited** mindset and a **limitless** mindset.

A limited mindset believes only a select few get an opportunity, and if that opportunity passes you by, there will be no more opportunities. Period. A limited mentality says that once you receive an amount of money, no more money will ever come in again. It also believes that if you're turned down for a scholarship that no other scholarship will ever come your way.

See how flawed that thinking is? It slams the door on believing that other opportunities exist. It dictates in your mind that one negative response, one disappointment is the end of the world. See the illusion of flawed, scarcity thinking?

Conversely, an unlimited mindset believes everyone should have an opportunity no matter their race, religion, creed, sexual orientation, or education. An unlimited mindset believes there are opportunities for all of us, because we create those opportunities. Anything you see in this world that's man-made, all started in a human being's mind.

When I think about my hometown, Dayton, Ohio, I think about the Wright brothers owning a bicycle shop. One day they had an idea to create a crazy monster flying machine.

The same goes for Henry Ford, Bill Gates, Steve Jobs, Richard Branson, and a myriad of others who thought beyond boundaries. None were superhuman people. They were human, like us, but they thought about creating something, and then they applied that thinking.

When you realize that the power of your thoughts can manifest something of gargantuan magnitude, you become free of restrictions. But if you think big ideas and achievements are only for a select few, then you're limited, and you'll never escape the shackles that you put on your mind…read that again…YOU put on your mind, because you're the only one who can attach those shackles. But once you unshackle your mind, and apply discipline, by remaining engaged in your own life, that's how you become limitless. It's very profound the more you think about it.

And I'm not just telling you the importance of a limitless mindset from a how-to perspective; I employ a limitless mindset in my own life on a daily basis. I decided at a young age that I wouldn't accept external roadblocks—I adopted the mentality of, how about I figure out *how* I can get this done, not *if* I can get this done. Edison found 1,000 ways not to make a light bulb but in the end he accomplished his goal. Patience and perseverance get the job done.

Mental Blocks that Hinder

Out of all the stakeholders, athletes specifically face unique mental blocks that prevent them from reaching their next playing level. We regularly witness within the basketball culture an athletic attitude that reeks of *my shit don't stink*. Young athletes are being doted over for a very superficial ability, an ability that will manifest itself for how long? A few years at best, before most of their names are forgotten for the new hot shots.

Guess what? You shooting a ball from half court isn't going to help provide water to Third World countries where people are going without water. That's not going to bring electricity to those that don't have electricity. That's not going to bring food to those here in the U.S. or abroad who don't have enough to eat.

Young athletes are being made to think they're better than they really are, that they're more than they really are. The NFL and NBA are businesses, entertainment, and you're a commodity for them. You have a unique skill set. Yes, but that doesn't make you better than anyone else. So, lack of humility is a major mental block.

Another major mental block is getting too caught up in outside influences like social media buzz. I'm putting on my agent hat right now, and being completely frank with you. Despite all the tweets, retweets, likes, and comments, it comes down to the fact that you must prove your ability to achieve what you do, not what others perceive your abilities to be. And we all know everybody has an opinion and is not shy about sharing it, especially behind the cloak of social media. The trick is to not let it guide and lead you. This is where tunnel vision is a good thing.

Previously, I talked about my not allowing external roadblocks to hinder me. That's not to say I haven't had to battle with mental blocks along the way. I grew up in the Midwest so I was most definitely aware of the African-American population and the Caucasian population. At the time, I bought into the limited mentality that white people could succeed, and black people couldn't.

I was being taught that same mindset in school. I remember very vividly during middle school, in Mr. Skittle's social studies class, learning about slavery and realizing everyone in the class was staring at me. I was taught that I'm property. I'm the descendent of property. Conclusion at the time? Clearly, I'm not going to be successful. Clearly, I'm not the smart one.

I had to ultimately stop caring about everyone's opinion. Stop caring about the past. The past is the past. I can't blame anyone who exists today for slavery, or for the past. What I learned is to hold everyone accountable for treating people with respect and dignity. Much of the ill-will that was present in the past is still present today and I refuse to accept that it's not, because the world still shows us every day that is it indeed prevalent. I learned to see people's opinions as just that. People's opinions. I learned that nothing can guide my life other than me.

I always like to say I'm the master of my fate, I'm the captain of my soul, and I think once I learned to free myself from others' views and how others thought I should live my life and just started living the life that I feel I was destined to live, that's how I learned to overcome the limited mentality imposed upon me as a youth.

Nothing good comes from being comfortable or complacent. It is when you're uncomfortable, and you're pushed to the edge, when your back is against the wall, that's when greatness occurs.

Another group that has been told they can't achieve at top levels are women. I want women to realize how much power, how much potential they have because once women realize their power, global dynamics are going to drastically shift. They are the givers of life. I was involved in my wife's labor for both of my sons' births, but I did not bring them to life. They did not form inside of me, and I did not carry them for nine months. So it just makes me so upset when women are discarded, disregarded, downgraded. And if it wasn't for three very powerful women in my life, I wouldn't be the asskicker I am today. My grandmother, my mother, and my wife all influenced me to be the man I am today.

My grandmother, unfortunately, passed away my first year of law school. My mother is a federal employee, and believes that someday I'm going to conform to a non-entrepreneurial lifestyle of getting paid every two weeks from a company who tells me what I'm worth. Even though I don't buy into that mindset, we're making progress to come to a meeting of the minds.

The third influential woman is my wife. I tell her that I always had this light shining in me, but she is the kerosene. She is the fuel that has amplified my life to the extreme. She gave me two little human beings that look to me for guidance on how to be men, so I won't fail, because they're here. My most important job now is to help these two little princes to realize their success. I'm running this race so that decades from now when I pass the baton to my children, they will see and realize that my wife and I have given them every opportunity for empowered thinking. I'm not trying to box them in, I'm trying to move every box they can see and I'm striving every day to be a living example.

My wife will tell you, I am not all that empathetic or even sympathetic. I'm trying to work on that. I'm not overly emotional. The reason I make that comment is because, I think in modern society we make it a matter of, Oh you gotta be Mr. Tough Man, an alpha male. Well, I'm a very type A alpha male type person. I'm a control freak. I was ingrained in good old-fashioned American culture, "hard work," *not* smart work.

But even with my flawed thinking that everything should be my way or the highway, I still recognize the power of the most important being in our lives, the woman.

The facts are: I'm a black man from a single-family home, and I moved from Hooked on Phonics to a law degree. I really struggled with learning how to read when I was a kid. I started a business. I have an amazing wife and two children, and I'm living in a city that ever since I was five years old I told the world I was going to be in, Los Angeles, California, chasing my dreams. Now, I'm in Los Angeles, California chasing my dreams.

All of that is to say it's because the cards were not dealt in my favor that I decided I was going to wait for the next deal. I was going to wait for the next hand and I was going to continue being strategic and execute, and not allow the limits that the world put on me to limit me. I use my blackness to my advantage.

I'm not saying all this to brag; I'm simply saying I created the dream I'm living when I was told all I was was property. Why the hell are we not all doing it? For me to get to this stage in life, I had to employ some mental tools for the journey, and if you want to progress in your life, so do you. Without mental strategies, we tend to get derailed, distracted, and detoured.

First, find a trusted person who cares about you. Who *deeply* cares. When you find that person, talk to them. Listen to them. Be vulnerable with them. That's something I think I'm learning more and more. How a person connects with another person is through vulnerability. No one wants to see that macho *I'm good, I can do anything, I can do everything, there's nothing tough in front of me* mentality. That's going to lead you to a sad place. Through engaging in honest, sincere, vulnerable conversations, all stakeholders will benefit in the mental toughness space.

Second, practicing mindfulness is an underrated yet powerful tool. Mindfulness includes meditating, journaling, and reading material that enriches your mind. Meditating helps me stay grounded and focused in the present moment. Through journaling I'm able to express myself in a productive way; when a thought or idea is rattling around in my brain and doesn't quite make sense, writing it down helps transfer that thought out of my brain and onto paper, then voila, it does make sense after all.

The first thing I do in the morning is prayer/meditation and I also read a portion of a book. Presently, I'm reading Tim Ferriss's *Tools of Titans* that looks at how successful people fail, how they succeed, what they think, and how they interact. I let that content wash over me as soon as I wake up.

Being an early riser, taking care of yourself, sharpening your mind through some of the practices I've mentioned is how you'll far exceed your own expectations. Putting these mental tools into practice will cause you to realize that you're good enough. You're okay.

And I know it sounds foo-foo, but once you really learn to accept and love and appreciate yourself, that's where something special happens. That's when circumstances start happening in your favor. Because you can't love others, you can't respect others if you don't love and respect yourself.

Remember, your central focus, your outlook, isn't coming from your mother, your sister, your brother, your wife, your coach, your teammate, your agent, your financial advisor, although they will be impacted because of your mind shift because they will see you walking that walk. Your focus, your outlook, comes from *your* mental toolbox.

As I've said, yes, glean tools from others you respect, but ultimately, your mental toolbox is for you, and someone else's toolbox is for them.

Mental toughness is many things, said famous Green Bay Packers coach Vince Lombardi. *It is humility because it behooves all of us to remember that simplicity is the sign of greatness and meekness is the sign of true strength. Mental toughness is spartanism with qualities of sacrifice, self-denial, and dedication. It is fearlessness, and it is love.* According to Lombardi, mental toughness is character in action.

In the final chapter of this book, we're going to finish strong with some key elements to mental toughness that will revolutionize the daily life of any stakeholder. Continue reading to steer into sturdy, stout territory for your mind.

Intersection of Education and Empowerment

Direction Questions:

On a scale of 1-10, how would you rate your level of mental toughness today, right now?

What mental blocks are hindering you from going to the next level? Acknowledge them, fear them, get mad at them, and then grieve their loss for a few moments because you will be continuing your journey without them.

Empowerment Exercise:

Review the qualities of the mentally tough and the ten action steps to become mentally tough. Make a list of your strongest qualities and your weakest qualities. Spend time developing your strongest qualities.

Choose one of the ten action steps and…well…take action!

GOAL EIGHT

Stay on Course toward Success with Mental Strength

"Success depends upon previous preparation, and without such preparation there is sure to be failure."

~Confucius

Let's turn our attention now to some of the various aspects of mental toughness and how stakeholders can put those aspects into play in order to advance, both personally and professionally.

Self-Confidence through Serving Others

Character in action commands that there is a tipping point between possessing self-confidence and being boastful and arrogant, and the line is often blurred. It comes down to removing judgment. When you have a degree of healthy self-confidence, you're not judging yourself, and you're not judging others. You simply buy in and believe in yourself. What harms us is buying into a boastful, conceited, negative mentality.

The best way all stakeholders can exercise self-confidence is to think about others as much as you think about yourself, even though at first glance that may seem counterintuitive. If you go into a situation thinking about how you can one-up someone, you very well may succeed, but that's not going to lead to the greatest result.

It might help to remember the line in the classic sports movie, Jerry Maguire, "Help me help you." My brother jokes about that very line. He says, "I would much rather someone be honest and tell me 'I'm going to help you because it helps me accomplish my own goal.'" However, a lot of people go into a conversation or situation thinking, *I'm going to take advantage of you and you're going to help me hit my goal* but they would never say that out loud.

Owning your self-confidence means you're concerned with how the other person benefits from a situation, not just yourself. Those who are out to make a bunch of money might gain a little bit at the onset, but most will fail in the end. But those whose mission is to solve problems will always succeed.

A natural byproduct of being mindful and conscious of other people is personal and professional success—you don't have to toil and strain—it will be a natural result. True harmonization comes from realizing that life is a constant series of negotiations, and it takes making concessions for anything to work. We all know people who live by the mantra, *my way or the highway*. We also know that they are not fun people to be around.

I heard a phrase growing up that said, "A man becomes a man when he realizes how he impacts others." I didn't really understand what that even meant until I had children and I realized that what I do for the good or the bad impacts them, so I have to always do my best. I have to see how I am influencing them for the good and for the bad, and I pray that I can mitigate the bad and amplify the good.

The following are crucial traits one must possess to "own" an empowered mindset. You're undoubtedly strong in some areas and maybe need a little boost in others. The idea is to allow each one to sink in to your soul; embrace each trait, hone the traits that don't come natural to you, and then go out and make a difference in others' lives.

Humility

The biggest benefit of being humble is that you're comfortable with yourself, and you aren't putting unnecessary pressure on yourself. By being humble, you're accepting yourself and realizing you're flawed, but you're also great.

Once you become self-aware enough to realize the flaws in yourself, it then allows you to realize that others have flaws, and therefore makes you much more tolerant of others' idiosyncrasies. It's also recognizing that others can be great too. So being humble lets you realize and understand yourself, which will then help you better understand other people. And that leads to the advancement of all.

Prudence

When I think of prudence, I think of structure. I think of organization. I think of being on top of things. It's by no means easy to be a prudent individual. Practicing prudence is not the easiest character trait to implement consistently. It's not always choosing the easy way but rather what is a little uncomfortable, a little out of your comfort zone. The ability to thrive in uncomfortable situations is what pushes all of us forward.

Self-regulation

Self-regulation is accountability. And by being accountable, you're understanding that you have responsibilities that you must live up to and you're aware that if you don't live up to those responsibilities, then you're not accountable and you're not regulating yourself. When situations don't work the way you want, you can't blame anyone else—self-regulating is understanding what you must do for yourself.

So what are you going to do to help yourself be accountable? What is your contribution? How are you going to be part of your solution instead of saying *Yeah, whatever happens, happens*?

You've got to own whatever slice of control or impact you possess because as you self-regulate, you'll not only benefit society, you'll benefit yourself. That's a far better option than to render yourself useless because you can't control your thoughts, your emotions, or your actions.

Resiliency

Resiliency contains fun results but is by no means fun when you're smack dab in the middle of a situation that will eventually yield resiliency. It gets fun when you come out the other side of the fire and realize *I got a couple of burns, but I didn't burn up*.

Resiliency helps advance all stakeholders because when it bears its fruit, you realize you're far greater than you ever imagined, and you're far more powerful than you ever thought you could be. Resiliency yields bumper crops of self-awareness and self-confidence. By developing resiliency you not only push yourself forward, you push everyone collectively forward by reshaping the dynamics of what is possible.

Roger Bannister accomplished that very thing when he broke the four-minute mile record. What happened afterward? Many others went on to run the four-minute mile because Roger set a new precedent. That's how innovation comes. That's how change comes. Don't accept limits. Set new limits. That's the power of resiliency.

Focus

Focus makes all the characteristics we're talking about possible. Focus takes consciousness, awareness, and being in tune with all that surrounds you and makes possible what you set out to achieve. Focus is saying what you're going to do, and then following it up with action.

Lucky for us, science has finally debunked the multitasking theory and we're all better for it. In the past, most every resume listed being a multitasker as a core competency and a sought-after skill, but science has consistently shown that the human brain can only sustain attention on one item at a time. Think of driving and texting.

A 15five.com[1] blog post says it well: "Some people pride themselves on being able to juggle multiple objectives at once. But when you do that, your mind is never really focused on any one task. It often happens that we meet a new person and instantly forget their name—that's because our minds are distracted and are unable to process or retain that new information."

The article goes on to say that multitasking has a negative impact on your short-term memory, causes anxiety, inhibits creativity, stops flow states, and halts living and enjoying

---

[1] Smith, Simone. "7 Reasons Why You Should Stop Multitasking and Actually Get Things Done." https://www.15five.com/blog/7-reasons-you-should-stop-multitasking/ (Accessed 9/19/2018).

life in the moment. They suggest putting your inbox on hold for at least a couple of hours, and I'll add to that and say for heaven's sake, take a break from your cell phone, let your fingers rest…you shall not surely die. Your eyes, fingers, and brain will thank you.

RealBuzz.com[2] highlights the following: Paul Dent, a London-based sports psychologist who has worked with Great British hockey team players, agrees about this need to focus on the present. He said: "The task is to focus on what you are doing, i.e. having a narrow attentional focus on the here-and-now—not the fact that millions of people are watching (which is a broad attentional focus) or the implications of missing (the future)."

Tenacity

Tenacity is the quality or fact of being able to grip something firmly. It's built brick by brick, decision by decision. I can either be tenacious or I can be cowardly. And if I'm going to be tenacious, it's going to require me to do X, Y, and Z; it sets the tone for how to conduct myself, which will either cause me to advance, or I will regress.

Choose tenacity! When most people are going through an especially challenging situation, their first thought is *how can I get out of this situation as soon as possible?* That's the starting point of giving up, yet we know nothing of value can come from throwing in the towel on a situation.

---

[2] Real Buzz. "Mental Strength in Sports." RealBuzz.com. https://www.realbuzz.com/articles-interests/sports-activities/article/mental-strength-in-sports/ (Accessed 9/19/2018).

Persistent Intensity

Persistent intensity means that you are dedicated, you are obsessed with accomplishing your goals. That persistence, that obsession, that intensity, that commitment to your goals is what separates you from the pack, and will be the fuel that gets it done. Persistent intensity is doing what needs to be done when you don't feel like doing it. Embody persistent intensity; allow it to wash over you daily. First it becomes a habit, then it becomes the standard.

Acclaimed author Stephen Covey succinctly lays out the path of persistent intensity in one of his wildly famous quotes: "Sow a thought, reap an action; sow an action, reap a habit; sow a habit, reap a character; sow a character, reap a destiny."

The current standard reveals the attitude of most: when things get a bit uncomfortable, just quit. After all, that's the easy way out, right? Well, it is if you want to move yourself straight into non-existence.

Goal-setting

Goal-setting is your road map to success. Say you're setting off on a road trip. You know what city you're going to, and the name of the hotel you're staying at, but you've never been to this particular city before. In today's age, we simply turn on our GPS, key in the destination address, and off we go. Before GPS, people would use Thomas Brothers map books for each city they wanted to visit, and I suppose before that were the near-impossible-to-fold-up paper maps. You needed some kind of plan to get to your destination, your travel goal.

My point is: If you don't know where you're going, you can't go anywhere. Goal-setting helps you know the direction you're moving in, and even if you don't reach that goal, guess what? You're a lot better off than not having goals at all.

Mental Rehearsal

When I was playing high school sports, I remember I tried to personify mental rehearsal, because it was said that Allen Iverson, who was still playing at that time, could see an entire game played in his head before he even played it.

Mental rehearsal is the belief, the optimistic view that what you want is real. But for it to be real in the world around you, it must first be real in your mind. Mental rehearsal allows you first and foremost to see that what you're striving for can be done. Like Allen Iverson, and countless others, once you view it as done in your mind, it's just a matter of carrying out the vision in your actions.

Self-Talk

Whether you realize it or not, you're always talking to yourself. I'm not talking about squirrely nut house talk, but rather the kind of self-talk you're constantly feeding your mind, all day every day. Unfortunately, most of us talk to ourselves in a negative way. We must be conscious of what we are telling ourselves and realize that our thoughts become our reality. Where you are today, what is in your world, is the direct result of your thoughts. If you don't like where you are, it's time to change your thoughts. Self-talk is that internal voice you turn to the right frequency in order to craft the life you want, the life vision for which you aspire.

Positive self-talk reinforces the fact that what you're going for is truly going to be your future even if it isn't your present.

Stimulation Control

When I talk about stimulation control, I'm talking about a player who is overly anxious going into a game, and as a result is unable to control his temper, or the outside stimulation of the crowd, whether cheering or booing, or the opposing team. I can tell you that you never want to be too high or too low — that's one big thing I've learned from successful athletes, and from people around sports.

You're going to take wins and you're going to take losses. Celebrate the wins, but don't be overly jubilant. Understand and analyze the losses, but don't dwell on them. By being even-keeled, by staying grounded and in the moment, and not being overly stimulated in one direction or the other, you'll be more focused, you'll be able to think more clearly, and you'll be able to make better decisions.

Stimulation control is the ultimate expression of being in the Now. Adonal Foyle says in his book *The Athlete CEO* that when he had a disappointing loss when he was playing with the Warriors, he would give himself a certain number of minutes, five minutes, to just rant or cry or whatever. Then he got over it and kept on steppin'.

I grew up in an environment where the unspoken rule was, if something bad happens, don't even acknowledge it. But that mentality doesn't solve the problem, it just delays it and makes it worse. You don't want to carry around mental baggage for any length of time because it will suck out energy that could be used for much more worthy endeavors.

Emotional Intelligence

The dictionary defines emotional intelligence as, "The capacity to be aware of, control, and express one's emotions, and to handle interpersonal relationships judiciously and empathetically."

Yes, it is that but it's also recognizing and accepting someone for the uniquely beautiful, creative human being that they are. Emotional intelligence allows you to connect with others, to understand them, to appreciate them, and that will then allow you to thrive in your professional life, because, of course, everyone wants to do business with people they respect and appreciate.

Emotional intelligence is an extremely powerful tool that doesn't come from a book per se. It's something you develop through practice.

You can be a highly educated person and lack emotional intelligence. You can be a high school dropout and possess an extraordinary amount of emotional intelligence. Read the definition again and see if it describes you right here, right now. If so, great. If not, there are ways to develop it.

According to skillsyouneed.com[3] there are two primary benefits to emotional intelligence over having a high IQ:

1. People with higher emotional intelligence find it easier to form and maintain interpersonal relationships and to 'fit in' to group situations.

---

[3] Skills You Need. "Emotional Intelligence." skillsyouneed.com. https://www.skillsyouneed.com/general/emotional-intelligence.html (Accessed 9/18/2018).

2. People with higher emotional intelligence are also better at understanding their own psychological state, which can include managing stress effectively and being less likely to suffer from depression.

It's often said that the A+ student will work for the C+ student someday because "book smart" intelligence will only get you so far. Renowned author Robert Kiyosaki talks about this very thing in his book, *Why "A" Students Work for "C" Students and "B" Students Work for the Government: Rich Dad's Guide to Financial Education for Parents*[4]. Kiyosaki expands on his belief that "the school system was created to churn out 'Es' / Employees... those "A Students" who read well, memorize well and test well... and not the creative thinkers, visionaries and dreamers—entrepreneurs-in-the-making... those "C Students" who grow up to be the innovators and creators of new ideas, businesses, applications and products."

Book intelligence is a tool that can be used to open doors of opportunity, but unfortunately, it is often the very thing that disconnects you, because if you have book smarts yet lack emotional intelligence, your ability to interconnect with those around you will be hampered. Emotional intelligence dictates that you have self-awareness, self-regulation, and motivation as well as interpersonal skills like empathy and being easy to talk to, trustworthy. To possess both IQ *and* EQ—now that's a powerful combination that will work well for you!

What's on paper and what's applied are never typically the same. On paper everyone says, *Oh man, he should be the*

---

[4] Kiyosaki, Robert. *Why "A" Students Work for "C" Students and "B" Students Work for the Government: Rich Dad's Guide to Financial Education for Parents."* Scottsdale, AZ: Plata Publishing; 2nd edition, 2013.

one, let's make him the president, let's make him the next CEO, he has a perfect resume. But how a company leader relates to and treats employees is far more important than perfect metrics on paper. Emotional intelligence is the application of brilliance, not the mere state of just being brilliant. It's one of those things where you can be great at something, but if no one wants to be associated with you, what's the point of being great?

Helpguide.org[5] contains a plethora of helpful articles on EQ. One article, Improving Emotional Intelligence (EQ), states, "As we know, it's not the smartest people that are the most successful or the most fulfilled in life. You probably know people who are academically brilliant and yet are socially inept and unsuccessful at work or in their personal relationships. Intellectual ability or your intelligence quotient (IQ) isn't enough on its own to be successful in life. Yes, your IQ can help you get into college, but it's your EQ that will help you manage the stress and emotions when facing your final exams. IQ and EQ exist in tandem and are most effective when they build off one another."

And, by the way, this concept does not just apply to sports; it spans all industries and all positions.

We've covered a lot in this chapter, and you may need to go back and read certain portions where you feel you could use some extra support. That's what this book is for: It's a resource guide to equip, educate, and empower you to flourish and succeed within the sports industry, and resource guides are meant to be just that, a resource you can use over and over again when you need a refresher.

---

[5] HelpGuide. "Improving Emotional Intelligence." Helpguide.org. https://www.helpguide.org/articles/mental-health/emotional-intelligence-eq.htm. (Accessed 9/19/2018).

Intersection of Education and Empowerment

Direction Questions:

Which crucial traits discussed in this chapter describes your present mindset?

If a blind person had access to your brain and mindset, what would they see?

Empowerment Exercise:

Write out a contract with yourself to focus only on the controllables in your life. Accept things you cannot control as they are.

List three top ways you can turn your present adversity into advantages.

CONCLUSION

The legacy I want to leave you with is that no matter who you are, what you have been doing, or where you would like to go, if you look at a situation from a problem-solving approach and put others first, you'll succeed at whatever you aspire to do. Success isn't just for a few individuals. Success is for everyone. But the true challenge is we must individually define that definition of success for ourselves, and not allow the world to shape it for us, but be willing to stand up and say *this is how I feel, this is what I believe in, and this is what I'm willing to do to obtain my definition of success.*

I want to be instrumental in shaping or re-shaping the way we look at ourselves and our daily life—that each unparalleled individual has something to offer the world.

This book is bigger than I—I'm just the person who put something out there. It has nothing to do with me. I have the mentality, if something's going to get done, or something needs to get done, why not me? I'm not going to sit around and wait for the government to fix it. I'm not going to sit around and wait for another agency to fix it. I'm not going to sit around and wait for another athlete, another sports league and/or team to make it happen. Something needs to be done, so I'm going to do my part. There's a difference between optimism and reality. I'm optimistically realistic.

My wife has taught me the value of honesty and transparency. I'm learning. I'm working and realizing that I should give people power and knowledge about myself because it helps them connect with me on a deeper level. If anyone thinks I'm not that scared little boy, it's merely because I try to hide that vulnerable part of myself, but that kid still lives inside me, and I imagine most of us. The difference is I'm trying to build my sons up each day to be strong yet transparent men.

Realize where we are today and take the steps to get where we must go tomorrow. I think that's kind of been the whole premise of accepting and realizing this is where I am today but go into tomorrow doing what you need to do, employing the practices that will make you fulfilled. Appreciating and loving and accepting yourself for where you are, educating and acting in a way that moves you where you want to go. I think that would be where I'd want the reader to just conclude and realize that we went on a very long journey, but realistically where we started and where we ended up are almost the same place.

We started by realizing this is the current state of affairs. We want to change those, and we learned about how we could change those in the middle, but really, we're right back at the end, we're in the beginning, and realizing these are the things we want to change, and this is the impact we need to have. We need to go back to the beginning and understand we must love and appreciate and respect ourselves, which will then allow us to love and appreciate and respect others, and act upon that love and appreciation and respect in a way that empowers, fulfills, sustains and provides ability to thrive for all of us.

I want to leave you with this: If I had super powers I would want the power to heal other people because I feel if we heal other people, those people will then want to heal others because of their own gratefulness for being healed. Within my ability to help solve problems, and to help heal my fellow human beings, my hope is that they in turn would go out and try to help and heal individuals, thus creating a continual pay it forward mentality. It's the power of multiplicity!

We all possess the power to heal in one way or another; whether with our smile, our wisdom, our practical skills, our knowledge, a gentle touch, or our encouraging, uplifting, empowering words. If we use our healing power to help others jump over the hurdles that life places in front of them, and then others use their own unique healing power to heal those surrounding them, the effects will reverberate throughout the world.

Empower others to empower the world!!!

ABOUT THE AUTHOR

Michael McGinnis grew up in Dayton, Ohio and continuously played sports until college, when he realized his passion for improving the lives of athletes through empowerment, education, and knowledge of the sports business model. Michael attended the University of Dayton and completed a Bachelor's in Sports Management with an emphasis in Entrepreneurship. He then went on to pursue a law degree while working with an MLB agent and taking on an advisory role with a start-up NBA agency, until he decided to start his own advisory and consulting business. Michael has worked on multi-million- and multi-billion-dollar contracts with the federal government, and now, with eight years of experience negotiating major contracts and advising athletes within the MLB and NBA systems, he has composed the quintessential manual to guide not only athletes and those who support them but anyone looking to make their break in professional athletics. He currently resides in Los Angeles, California with his wife and two sons.

ACKNOWLEDGEMENTS

Thank you is not enough to express my appreciation for my wife, my sons, my mother, and my brothers who have always stood with me and given me a reason to stand for what I believe in.

Spending time with my frat brothers, Kappa Alpha Psi, Iota Mu Chapter, is where I learned the value of having the right team.

I owe a debt of gratitude to all my University of Dayton Sports Management Professors and Advisors. They lit the spark and helped the flame grow.

I would not be the business person I am today without my business mentors, Mark Allen and Everett Glenn. You both have consistently shared your keen insight and guidance with me, and I am a better man for it.

My profound appreciation and admiration goes to Gladys West, a "hidden figure" known for her mathematical genius, and a pivotal member of the original team that created the world-changing GPS system. Still going strong at eighty-seven, in 2018 Gladys was inducted into the United States Air Force Hall of Fame and completed her PhD via a distance-learning program with Virginia Tech. Gladys, you are truly my inspiration for the book title!

Thank you to all my business associates who I have interacted with in any capacity on the voyage to getting my book done. This includes Michelle Hill, *Your Legacy Builder* at Winning Proof, my book collaborator. Without her help and guidance you would not be holding this book in your hands. Michelle and her team provided the headlights that got me to my destination: Michael Scott, thank you for creating a captivating cover design; Michael LaRocca, for your expert proofreading and editing; Fred Vinson, for building me a website I can be proud to display; and last but not least, my publisher, Drew Becker, owner of Realization Press, for your expertise, knowledge, and dedication to making this book a work of art.

HOW TO ORDER

To secure Michael McGinnis to *provide advisory services* for you as an athlete, or to *book* Michael for your next team, employee, or leadership meeting, conference, retreat, or convention, to *order single or bulk copies*, or to *request media interviews*:

Website: empowersportsgroup.com/book

Email:) michael@empowermentsportsgroup.com

Phone: (424) 229-1504

If you're a fan of this book please tell others...

- Write about *G.P.S. Guide For Athletes and Those Who Surround Them* on your blog and social media channels.

- Suggest this book to your friends, family, neighbors, and coworkers.

- Write a positive review on Amazon.com.

- Purchase additional copies for your business or sports team, or to give away as gifts.

- Feature Michael on your radio or television broadcast.

Good-bye (English)

Adios (Spanish)

Aloha (Hawaiian)

Arrivederci (Italian)

Au revoir (French)

Auf Wiedersehen (German)

Shalom (Hebrew)

Totsiens (African)

Vale (Latin)

Zaijian (Chinese)

www.ingramcontent.com/pod-product-compliance
Lightning Source LLC
Chambersburg PA
CBHW071330110526
44591CB00010B/1090